Bioethical
Decision-Making

Bioethical Decision-Making

*releasing religion
from the spiritual*

by
Barbara Ann
DeMartino Swyhart

FORTRESS PRESS   Philadelphia

Library of Congress Catalog Card No. 75–13040

ISBN 0-8006-0418-0

5107G75   Printed in the United States of America   1-418

In memory of "our" fathers,

JOSEPH JOHN DEMARTINO, JR.

and

CARL ARTHUR SWYHART

Contents

Preface

Bioethical Decision-Making: Releasing Religion from the Spiritual represents six years of probing the issues raised by the meeting of ethics and religion. Its motivation has been my students of ethics at Chestnut Hill and LaSalle Colleges, Philadelphia, Pennsylvania, as well as at San Diego State University, San Diego, California. Relating to men and women in the anxiety-producing decision-making process in areas that affect the most intimate aspects of their lives caused me to reflect on the process of decision-making itself.

The suggestion for the pursuit of this work comes exclusively from the confident counsel of the Fortress Press staff. I am indebted to Eugene Fontinell, professor of philosophy, Queens College, New York, whose work has encouraged and guided my thinking toward the application of relational, process thinking to concrete problems.

Although my contact with the Center for Process Studies, Claremont, California, has been infrequent, the suggestion of John Cobb and David Griffin to apply the thought of Alfred North Whitehead to the practical areas of ethics, psychology, and related fields has strongly influenced me. However, I must admit that my first intention is not Whiteheadian interpretation but rather a reshaping of the constructs suggested by process thinking—notably, although not exclusively, Whiteheadian—toward decision-making.

A research grant from the San Diego State University Foundation made it possible for me to attend the Institute of Society, Ethics, and the Life Sciences. With the help of Daniel Callahan, its director, the associates and staff, abstract ethics was made concrete and relational. I am particularly grateful for the work of Arthur J. Dyck, Mary B. Saltonstall Professor of Population Ethics, Harvard School of Public Health, member of the faculty of the Divinity School, and member of the Center for Population Studies. He has kindly given me permission to quote from his study, *Religious Views and United States Population Policy: Documentary Studies.* This was prepared for the Commission on Population Growth and the American Future by the Population Task Force of the Institute of Society, Ethics, and the Life Sciences, 1971.

The construct "'meeting" of Martin Buber, taught to me by Maurice Friedman, has engendered the novel re-creation of its use; the construct "paradox," as suggested by Reinhold Niebuhr and Paul Tillich, has created the problematic of the "meeting" of individual and social ethics. Both constructs were seminally brought together in my doctoral dissertation "Value Ontology: An Evaluation of Mordecai M. Kaplan's Philosophy of 'Wisdom'" (supported by a fellowship from the American Association of University Women, 1971–72). But constructs are not ends in themselves. In ethics, particularly bioethics, and decision-making, each construct is only an operational form beginning the process of decision-making. *Bioethical Decision-Making,* too, is another beginning.

My sincere thanks are extended to Rebecca Wheeler at the Word Processing Center of San Diego State University for the patient typing of the manuscript. To Mark Lester and George Edge, my able research assistants, I extend personal gratitude for their labors.

But a response of lasting value makes it all worthwhile. For this I thank my husband Paul.

BARBARA ANN DeMARTINO SWYHART

San Diego, California
January 5, 1975

Introduction

The Emerging Ethician

Good decision-making . . . seems to require human sensitivity, illuminating and useful principles, access to pertinent information, methods of weighting and balancing options—reason and feeling, private meditation and public discussion, good sense and good sensibilities.[1]

Religious ethics in the seventies demands "concretization." It depends on the sciences and the practical arts for its theoretical grounding and for its application. The once leisurely discipline of ethics now begins where man is—in the complex of technocratic society. Religious, ethical philosophy requires a more concrete perceptual experience of such concepts as "soul," "salvation," and "morality." Concretization means that religious ethics must reappraise man and the philosophy of *technique* prevalent in our world. (As is often the case in a philosophical work, the use of the word "man" is generic.) Religious ethics must be framed in an operational hypothesis. "The true meaning of a term is to be found by observing what a man does with it, not by what he says about it."[2] As a philosophic form, religious ethics is being reconstructed to operate for the holistic man—past, present, and future. It has moved away from the metaphysical hierarchy into the ontological status of the *logos* to achieve adequate responses of value to the social technological world.

Since our modern model of religious ethics is a modified operationalism, ethics has been nurtured in a fertile field of functional value within the regenerated aspects of human living in the seventies. These aspects of living include the sociological, anthropological, psychological, and medical models, as well as the traditional philosophical and religious models of human and divine meaning. Religious ethics is further influenced by economics. Economics is a study of man's attempt to grapple with the costs and benefits which are part of the behavior patterns of individuals and institutions.[3] *Within* the limits of dilemmas seemingly fragmented aspects of human life open up to the ethician, and, *without* (outside of) these limits, in the yet uncovered, novel possibilities suggested by the concrete ethical issues, the philosopher, or the religionist, as ethician is concerned with the practical areas demanding the guidelines of some decision-making process. In the area of bioethics, for example, are the traditional perceptions of the concepts of "soul," "body," "life," "death," adequate to respond constructively with value to the biomedical information which is being tested and in many cases presently operates without the a priori clear lines of "right and wrong"? One instance of a predicament without such a guide is the ethical question of "abortion." What I am going to suggest is that the emerging ethician cannot merely rest comfortably in one discipline to suggest an ethic for many aspects of the human individual and the human family. An interdisciplinary approach must be the starting point of a discussion of any ethical problematic raised by a technocracy.

Mindful of the dangers as well as the assets of any interdisciplinary professional approach to ethics, the ethician must work within the area of "what is" to create "what will be," and not vice versa. He is concerned with a wholly integrated (organic) method of decision-making, offering to man the options which advanced knowledge has made possible. "Ethician" is the construct I have selected to illustrate the task of one who does ethics, drawing on philosophical, religious, and medical resources. In contrast to the term "ethicist" widely being used in the discipline of bioethics, "ethician" suggests the activity of an academic practitioner who, by training and acumen, is able to do ethics in the complex situations of current medical ethics. Ethician suggests the professsion of a process-oriented rather than substance-oriented discipline. He is more than an ethics counselor; less than a therapist (in the psychological dimension); more than a pastoral counselor in

2

terms of his neutral epistemological parameters, and finally, less than a dogmatist in the academy. The ethician "sees" with an imagination describable as a multidimensional paradoxical process in which ontology itself is revelatory and being human is the quest. We have yet to educate such an imagination. To begin this task I intend to stir our thinking about the role of the ethician within a reshaped understanding of religion and the ethical paradox. These options are offered with the primary concern of man's ethical well-being. I believe that a framework of an operational, process ethics offers possibilities for such options. Process ethics assumes that man is constantly *becoming* holistic through a continuity of thought and action. I acknowledge that medical, legal, psychological, and religious issues concerning his development are variables, subject to the knowledge of our technocratic and scientific advances. The much needed cooperation among the humanities, arts, and sciences for a holistic vision is aptly described by Alfred North Whitehead, in *Science and the Modern World*:

> . . . the celibacy of the medieval learned class has been replaced by a celibacy of the intellect which is divorced from the concrete contemplation of the complete facts. . . . The remainder of life is treated superficially, with the imperfect categories of thought derived from one profession.
>
> The dangers arising from this aspect of professionalism are great, particularly in our democratic societies. The directive force of reason is weakened. The leading intellects lack balance. They see this set of circumstances, or that set; but not both sets together. The task of coordination is left to those who lack either the force or the character to succeed in some definite career. In short, the specialized function of the community is performed better and more progressively, but the generalized direction lacks vision. The progressiveness in detail adds only to the danger produced by the feebleness of coordiantion. This criticism of modern life applies throughout, in whatever sense you construe the meaning of community. It holds if you apply it to a nation, a city, a district, an institution, a family, or even to an individual. There is a development of particular abstractions and a contraction of concrete appreciation. The whole is lost in one of its aspects. It is not necessary for my point that I should maintain that our directive wisdom, either as individuals or as communities, is less now than in the past. Perhaps it has

slightly improved. But the novel pace of progress requires a greater force of direction if disasters are to be avoided. . . . We are left with no expansion of wisdom and with greater need of it.[4]

The wisdom expressed in this passage must begin in the *process* of human living. The reaches of consciousness can then move to the realm of ontological concerns. Ontology is suggested by the revelation of imaginative experience.

> The social function of religion is thus not only the expression and cultivation of what men together hold worthwhile, the celebration of their values. *It is also to clarify what men really want to extend and deepen their values, to set their transitory enthusiasms in a broader perspective.*[5]

Many hopeful believers presume that religion is merely in a state of transition. A myriad of images, concepts, current institutional changes, and new fringe groups pervade the American religious scene. This period of transition has its questioning, its critical evaluation of ideas and leaders, and its open discussions of the religious moral views which, before approximately the last thirteen years, were quietly passed from one generation to the next, and leaves religious morality in a state of ambiguity. However, these hopefuls are too presumptuous. This is not merely a period of transition, but rather a stage in the ongoing, processive religious development of man. Man has asserted a new place for himself, a place of "decision-making participation," within the realm of nature. This new-found being, man-the-decision-maker, is in need of education regarding his options, including possibilities and limitations, in order to participate adequately in his reality.

Many adventurers have embarked upon the philosophical, theological, and religious probe of this transitional stage experienced by American religious moralists.[6] In the process some notable changes have taken place. The *divine* qualities of love, forgiveness, balance in nature and society have been delegated to man as a doer. Divinity has been "verbed" (i.e, moved from a substantive to a functional construct) to supply the continuous novel operations of man the doer. Dr. Callahan, presently the director of the Institute of Society, Ethics, and Life Sciences, the Hastings Center, wrote in 1968:

> If as the Jewish and the Christian traditions hold, man is made in the image of God, then we do no disservice to God by fashioning our concept of him from what we know of man. Indeed, we may do a distinct disservice to God if we continue to insist that he is unattainable mystery; for that is to doom God to isolation, making a mockery of the powers God himself supposedly gave man. The problem of God today is not to deepen the mystery of God, but to get to the bottom of it. If God is to remain a mystery, then mankind will be left to its own resources anyway. It is as plausible to adopt as a working hypothesis that man is the mystery as it is to locate the mystery in God.[7]

Through process thought we have witnessed a transition from a totally transcendent God to an immanent, functioning "divining" process.

These adventurers have further discovered that man is a paradox of conflicting interests. He is the war-maker and the peacemaker; the lover and the violent hater; the rationale for life and the destroyer of its long-lived traditions; the creator of the structured systems of belief and the vocal disbeliever in structure. The justification for such a puzzling discovery is not so easy as the surface description of man I have rendered. Contemporary thinkers have come face-to-face with that hard fact also. The justifications offered in the name of love, in the name of the person, in the name of the welfare of the community have been unconvincing to institutional systems whose existence depends upon the economic dialectic on concrete issues between the institution (including its ideology) and its constitutents.[8] The need for a new methodology for the reconstruction of values arises from the *continuous strain* of involvement which religious traditions in the past have brought to us. While religious traditions have been punctuated by periodic restatements of religious truth, this continuous strain of involvement is an attempt to reinterpret the meaning of religion in terms of existing religious structures modified by popular and technological culture,[9] as if religion were other than the culture in which it develops and prospers. I will argue that this perspective is fail-

5

ing because religion cannot be the source of its own novelty. It cannot because: (1) religion—as a term used to designate a particular tradition—has taken on a radical meaning of immanent transcendence;[10] (2) culture is the key to the description of religion;[11] (3) ethics is the core of religion; (4) man is the focal point of all that history, biblical literature, current advances in physics, biology, and psychosocial phenomena have revealed. In summary, wisdom—and not faith—is the core of religion. Theology as the particular *logos* of correlation between God and man by faith is insufficient to religious ethics. Religious education must, therefore, be concerned with the wisdom of man and mankind first, and with faith as a posterior act of wisdom.[12] Faith is *derived from* the wisdom of man's "rational" functional activity. Professor Whitehead in his discussion of the nature and importance of the role of philosophy in science in the modern world implies that faith springs from the harmony of nature itself.

> Faith in reason is the trust that ultimate natures of things lie together in a harmony which excludes mere arbitrariness. It is the faith that at the base of things we shall not find mere arbitrary mystery. The faith in the order of nature which has made possible the growth of science is a particular example of a deeper faith. This faith cannot be justified by any inductive generalization. It springs from direct inspection of the nature of things as disclosed in our own immediate present experience. There is no parting from your own shadow. To experience this faith is to know that in being ourselves, we are more than ourselves: to know that our experience, dim and fragmentary as it is, yet sounds the utmost depths of reality: to know that detached details merely in order to be themselves demand that they would find themselves in a system of things: to know that this system includes the harmony of logical rationality, and the harmony of aesthetic achievement: to know that, while the harmony for logic lies upon the universe as an iron necessity, the aesthetic harmony stands before it as a living ideal molding the general flux in its broken progress toward finer, subtler issues.[13]

A *systematic appraisal* of "what is" coupled with a *relational insight* into "what is" is conducive to the efficient operation of wisdom, culminating in the act of faith in the total process itself. Precision and accuracy are demanded in the concretization of religious ethics. Religious ethics binds the "stuff" of man and the cosmos in an action-oriented role of relating to and dealing with issues which have heretofore been taken for granted. Issues, such as biomedical concerns, power politics (Watergate), testing integrity, honesty, and courage—the virtues we *presume* to have permanent reality—and the meaning and intention of the "self" in the midst of direct and indirect societal pressures, are the "finer and subtler issues" of our particular time of novelty.

Novelty must be a perspective which seriously *reshapes paradigms* and builds operable constructs, and not merely reinterprets traditions. Novelty demands a resetting of the parameters of the total picture of man as religious.[14]

For a religious ethician to embark upon an explanation of this new life, i.e., an innovative plan for the continuation of man's productive being, is to proclaim himself creator of values amid changing priorities, and, at the same time, a threat to existing "institutionalism," as well as conventional and/or accepted ideas. This adventure challenges all that everyday man holds securely in his mind and in his imagination. The task demands a "value" reconstruction[15] of thought systems, a reshaping of paradigms, and creation of operable constructs, as well as a rethinking of the dialectical processes by which men live.[16] It requires the uprooting of the daily pattern of "lived truth," even if that "lived truth" is cast aside as merely a product of psychological, sociological, or any other need. These wants or needs must be satisfied holistically, not partially, in order to respond cognitively, emotionally, and actively to life. These needs are biological, including the contentment of sustenance, security, health, and sex; psychosocial needs, including sympathy, approval, cooperation, and influence which create the effective human being. Spiritual needs are also important, including direction within an ethico-religious people.[17]

Utilizing the "operational" philosophy as defined by Professor P. W. Bridgman and Sir Arthur Eddington,[18] i.e., that concepts should be defined in terms of experiential observation, teams of professionals are working toward the inclusion of interdisciplinary research and communication in the role of decision-making on the societal level. These research models, I believe, will offer basic learning paradigms for effective educational rehabilitation of man in the seventies and eighties with regard to the changing nature of even the religious itself. In the words of an American religionist, John Herman Randall, Jr., a quality or a value "would then not be a unique 'way of being,' but rather it would be what it does."[19] These qualities or values are discoverable by an operational methodology.

Possibilities of renewed religious thought possess no criterion of absolute certainty. There is no threat and no promised reward of mythological and untouchable metaphysical realities. Religious thought today is a restless adventure into the ethical paradox and probes the minds and hearts of individuals, of corporate groups, of systems, and of ideologies. The religious endeavor is defined by Clifford Geertz as "a system of symbols which acts to establish powerful, pervasive, and long-lasting moods and motivations in men by formulating conceptions of a general order of existence and clothing these conceptions with such an aura of factuality the moods and motivations seem uniquely realistic."[20] The functionally economic considerations of the whole man foster the religious endeavor. "Religion is a matter for the whole man and the full man, not for the specialized part of him. It is for this reason perhaps that specialization is in itself somewhat inimical to religion; the man who throws his whole being into the narrow channel of a single specialty, be it chemistry or economics, is quite apt to be hostile, or at least indifferent, to the great generalities of the spiritual and moral life."[21] In quoting this truth from Professor Boulding, I am not admitting that religion is not specific in its content and relationship to the practical, ethical, and moral issues of the time. Rather, I am suggesting that while religion is indeed for the full man, it is also, paradoxically, called into question only on specific issues and not on general issues, specific issues such as abortion, amnesty, and liberation which speak to multiple levels of ethical discourse. A clear statement of the problematic of multiple levels, which I have termed "the ethical paradox," is articulated in one form by Paul Tillich:

> [It is] the false assumption that the moral principle refers to the community in the same way that it refers to the personality.

But the structure of the community, including its structure of centeredness, is qualitatively different from that of the personality. The community is without complete centeredness and without the freedom which is identical with being completely centered. The confusing problem of sound ethics is that the community consists of individuals who are bearers of the spirit, whereas the community itself, because of its lack of a centered self, is not.[22]

It is further articulated by Reinhold Niebuhr in *Moral Man and Immoral Society*:

What is lacking among . . . moralists, whether religious or rational, is an understanding of the brutal character of the behavior of all human collectives, and the power of self-interest and collective egoism in all intergroup relations. Failure to recognize the stubborn resistance of group egoism to all moral and inclusive social objectives inevitably involves them in unrealistic and confused political thought. They regard social conflict either as an impossible method of achieving morally approved ends or as a momentary expedient which a more perfect education or a purer religion will make unnecessary. They do not see that the limitations of the human imagination, the easy subservience of reason to prejudice and passion, and the consequent persistence of irrational egoism, particularly in group behavior, make social conflict an inevitability in human history, probably to its very end.[23]

In *Bioethical Decision-Making* I intend to articulate an extrapolated version of the paradox that both Professors Niebuhr and Tillich detail and apply the paradox to the issue of religion, ethics, and spirituality, as well as to bioethics. Whether or not you agree with Niebuhr's or Tillich's response to the paradox, I do believe that both have given a leading clue to the inability of religious morality and existing normative forms of decision-making such as the "love ethic" to rescue "radial man"[24] from the pursuit of ethical idols. Both have raised the question of freedom.

When we are concerned with the ethical decision-making we are *not* dealing with an individual who necessarily wants to behave ethically. Rather, we are dealing with transcendent "technocratic" man who has no "I" which can be spoken of holistically by the ethician.[25] Further, we are relating to what Rollo May,

9

Silvano Arieti, and Walter Kaufman and others have called the disfunction of the will.[26] Man's search for meaning amid the meaningless can result in a functional creation of resolutions to his conflicts in the form of the maintenance of flexible tension. These resolutions have been presented in the form of de-ontological ethical theory;[27] bioethical theory;[28] psychotherapeutic techniques;[29] situational sexuality;[30] Eastern influence on the reconstruction of religious motivation.[31] I shall attempt to set in context a methodological framework for the understanding of these responses in the light of educational rehabilitation, that is, learning to use imagination: (1) to think crtically and novelistically; (2) to create dynamic fields of operability to reshape religious paradigms and form philosophical constructs; (3) to develop a self-style for decision-making in the areas of biomedical concerns and self-awareness. This methodological framework outlines the problematic and establishes the epistemological parameters of our construct "operational process." What are the constitutents of knowledge which support this hypothesis? For without the parameters of knowledge man is forced into unlimited license thus denying the reality of his ontological status. The problematic of decision-making and the ontological reality of man as individual and social, linked by the ambiguous category "personal," make up the sociological model of the problem.

Thus, the purposes of *Bioethical Decision-Making: Releasing Religion from the Spiritual* include: (1) the reshaping of religious paradigms and philosophical constructs relating to the physical and psychological development of man and woman as they are operative in the ethical life; (2) the maintenance of a continuing dialogue between the humanities and sciences regarding the quality of human life and development; (3) a contribution to the educational rehabilitation of those who are wrestling with structural, personal, and/or societal impotence; (4) the provision of a foundational methodology emphasizing process thought and value ontology (my term) which may be a clearing ground for pluralistic forms of religious ethics; (5) the illustration of the operational process in bioethics, especially relating to the problematic of abortion in particular, and to bioethics in general.

The Emerging Ethician

NOTES

1. Daniel Callahan, "Values, Facts and Decision-making," *Hastings Center Report*, I, no. 1 (June 1971).

2. P. W. Bridgman, *The Logic of Modern Physics* (New York: Macmillan. 1927), p. 7.

3. See Kenneth E. Boulding, *Beyond Economics: Essays on Society, Religion and Ethics* (Ann Arbor: University of Michigan Press, 1970).

4. Alfred North Whitehead, *Science and the Modern World* (New York: Macmillan, 1925), pp. 197–198.

5. John Herman Randall, Jr., *The Meaning of Religion for Man* (New York: Harper Torchbooks, 1970 [Introduction to Torchbook ed., 1968] originally published by Macmillan, 1946), p. 7. Italics mine.

6. Three adventurers who have explored the function of man as a participant in the creation of forms of responsibility are John Macquarrie, *Three Issues in Ethics* (New York: Harper & Row, 1972); Gibson Winter, *Elements for a Social Ethic* (New York: Macmillan, 1966 [1968]); and H. Richard Niebuhr, *The Responsible Self: An Essay in Christian Moral Philosophy*, with an introduction by James M. Gustafson (New York: Harper & Row, 1963).

7. Daniel Callahan, "Human Experience and God: Brightman's Personalistic Theism," in *American Philosophy and the Future; Essays for a New Generation*, ed. Michael Novak (New York: Charles Scribner's Sons, 1968), p. 243.

8. See Boulding, *Beyond Economics*, "Some Contributions of Economics to Theology and Religion," pp. 218–226.

9. Examples of this may be found in Richard King's "The Eros Ethos: Cult in the Counter Culture," *Psychology Today*, no. 3 (August 1972), pp. 35–70; Hans Jonas, "Technology and Responsibility: Reflections on the New Task of Ethics," in *Religion and the Humanizing of Man*, ed. James M. Robinson (Waterloo, Ontario: Council on the Study of Religion, 1972), pp. 1–19; Theodore Roszak, *The Making of a Counter-Culture: Reflections on the Technocratic Society and Its Youthful Opposition* (New York: Doubleday [Anchor], 1968); Theodore Roszak *Where the Wastelands Ends: Politics and Transcendence in Post Industrial Society* (New York: Doubleday [Anchor], 1973).

10. See *Transcendence*, ed. Cutler and Richardson (Boston: Beacon Press, 1969); Roszak, *Making of a Counter Culture*; Alistair Kee, *The Way of Transcendence: Christian Faith without Belief in God* (Baltimore: Penguin Books, 1971).

1. Cf. Paul Tillich, *Systematic Theology*, vol. III (Chicago: University of Chicago Press, 1963), pp. 11–50, 157–161, and 245–268.

12. Cf. Mordecai M. Kaplan, *The Religion of Ethical Nationhood* (New York: Macmillan, 1970).

13. Whitehead, *Science and the Modern World*, p. 18.

14. See Chapter II for a discussion of the epistemological parameters of decision-making.

15. I am indebted to Eugene Fontinell for his use of the construct "reconstruction." See *Toward a Reconstruction of Religion: A Philosophical Probe* (New York: Doubleday, 1970).

16. Cf. Ian G. Barbour, Langdon Gilkey, Thomas S. Kuhn, cited in Chapter III.

17. Dr. Mordecai M. Kaplan, in his philosophy of reconstructionism, outlines the basic needs of man, individually and socially, which constribute to the development of Jewish civilization, and which religion must satisfy; "The Thirteen Principles of the Society for the Advancement of Judaism" given at the dinner and dedication of the SAJ house, December 13, 1925. See also his *The Religion of Ethical Nationhood*, pp. 77–94. Abraham Maslow, in his description of deficiency needs, stated that before man can approach self-actualization he must satisfy basic needs. Cf. *Toward a Psychology of Being*, 2d ed. (New York: Van Nostrand Reinhold, 1968).

18. Cf. Bridgman, *The Logic of Modern Physics*, p. 5; also Sir Arthur Eddington, *The Mathematical Theory of Relativity* (London: Cambridge University Press, 1924), p. 3. Although both men relate to physical activities interpreted quantitatively, they also include "mental operations." They further recognize that within scientific theories two sorts of concepts are involved: (1) those measurable and operationally defined; (2) those which enter into theories as part of the apparatus for correlating observations.

19. John Herman Randall, Jr., *Nature and Historical Experience: Essays in Naturalism and in the Theory of History* (New York: Columbia University Press, 1958), p. 276.

20. Clifford Geertz, as quoted by Robert Bellah in *Beyond Belief: Essays in a Post-Traditional World*, (New York: Harper & Row, 1970), p. 12.

21. Boulding, *Beyond Economics*, p. 179.

22. Paul Tillich, *Systematic Theology*, III, p. 41, cf. II, p. 92.

> That is paradoxical which contradicts the *doxa*, the opinion which is based on the whole of ordinary human experience, including the empirical and the rational. . . . The "offense" given by the paradoxical character of the Christian message is not against the laws of understandable speech but against man's ordinary interpretation of his predicament with respect to himself, his world, and the ultimate underlying both of them. It is an offense against man's unshaken reliance upon himself, his self-saving attempts, and his resignation to despair.

23. Reinhold Niebuhr, *Moral Man and Immoral Society* (New York: Charles Scribner's Sons, 1932), p. xx.

24. See Richard R. Niebuhr, *Experimental Religion* (New York: Harper & Row, 1972), Chapter 2, "Human Faith, Radial World."

> To begin with the most general statement about this world/age, we have to say that what is salient in it is power. It is power in which we live and move and have our physical being. It is power which moves in, with, and under our personalities as we meet and part in this great field of action. It is power from which we flee and to which we run, from which we come and into which we vanish, which we admire and abhor. In our own idiom, we may say that our humanity stands and continually redresses its balance in a radial world. For the individual of this world/age lives in a vortex of rays and waves of light, of sound, of electricity—in short—of particles of energy. To be born is, for this man, to be endowed with power and the conatus for power. To love is to discern and approve the fitting

order of powers. To work is to learn a limited management of the power available to one. To die is to succumb to power. In a radial world we have our being as radial men.

Our world, however, is not merely power as such but displays toward, and works on, our humanity in two principal ways: to enlarge us and to make us small. By persuasion and by coercion [p. 28].

See also P. Teilhard de Chardin's use of the construct "radial energy," *The Phenomenon of Man*, trans. Bernard Wall, with an introduction by Sir Julian Huxley (New York: Harper & Row, 1961). First published as *Le Phénomène humain* (Paris: Editions du Seuil, 1955).

25. Cf. Roszak, *The Making of a Counter-Culture*, and Jacques Ellul, *The Technological Society* (New York: Random House [Vintage Books], 1964).

26. Rollo May, *Love and Will* (New York: W. W. Norton, 1969); *Power and Innocence: A Search for the Sources of Violence* (New York: W. W. Norton, 1972); Silvano Arieti, *The Will to Be Human* (New York: Quadrangle Books, 1972); Walter Kaufman, *Without Guilt and Justice: From Decidephobia to Autonomy* (New York: Peter H. Wyden, 1973).

27. See Niebuhr, *The Responsible Self* and Gibson Winter, *Elements for a Social Ethic* (New York: Macmillan, 1968 [1966]). Niebuhr offers man an "ethic of response" which is supposed to be de-ontological but in reality it is rooted in a theology of Christ recorded in the Appendix. Professor Winter, in his phenomenological approach to ethics, approaches a response of value but he is limited by the static environmental structure he creates. A response of value cannot be behavioral. It cannot be labeled in its *modus vivendi* a priori; nor can it be justified by reference to a universalized Christ. Finally, although man seeks the environmental constituents, a response of value is not solely created by the environmental structure.

28. As an example, see Chapter IV for a review of the literature pertaining to the issue of religion and abortion.

29. Cf. William Glasser, *Reality Therapy* (New York: Harper & Row, 1965).

30. See Joseph Fletcher, *Situation Ethics: The New Morality* (Philadelphia: Westminster Press, 1966). A recent work, *The Ethics of Genetic Control* (New York: Doubleday [Anchor], 1974), modifies the motivation of "love" by the motivation of "need." "In this book it will be held that if any act or policy is the wisest as measured by human need and well-being, then it is *positively* good, *positively* the right thing to do," p. 31.

31. See Jacob Needleman, *The New Religions* (Garden City, N.Y.: Doubleday, 1970).

I

The Ethical Paradox:
The Meeting of the Individual,
the Personal, and the Social

We talk about the concepts of human nature, the qualities of willing the good or the destructive, but we seldom rise to the level of considering values operationally in the concrete situations where decisions are required. We have difficulty weaving the dynamic human qualities of hope, pain, suffering, and joy into a normative frame. The theological sciences have erred in their all-embracing search for a concept of human nature that is somehow transcendent of all particular men. In focusing ethical scrutiny on the act in isolation from its network of intrication and implication and its natural and technological aspect, the philosophic tradition of ethics also leaves us floundering for value insights in a technological society.[1]

An age of "survival" demands the reshaping of paradigms out of which the process of decision-making occurs and the confronting of a basic problem, i.e., the problem of the insufficiency of an individual decision-making process to change or solve the dilemmas which confront man as a social being. Since religious paradigms have not confronted the dilemma of the individual meeting the society as two separate ontological realities, many of the religious paradigms are inoperative today in concrete issues. In the sixties the concept "alienation" spawned models which quickly evaporated due to the challenging problems which came from the new advances in medicine, biology, politics attendant to a changing technocracy. The personal and the social have collided in both the philosophical and the practical areas in conflicts of human freedom and personal needs with social constraints, of personal mobility with social structure, of communal immaterialism with economic structure. I contend that the use of a modified operationalism, including the adoption of workable constructs, as a method for decision-making, may be one way of allowing the personal or individual to meet the social in a manner which permits the integrity of each distinct area of human enterprise to remain. Only the myths surrounding an idealized person in society which characterized the existentialism of the sixties disappear.

A construct, according to the physicist P. W. Bridgman, consists of: (1) the unique correlation between a corresponding set of operations (i.e., concept) and the physical data in terms of which it is defined; (2) a connection with other physical phenomena, independent of those which entered into its definition.[2] The use of the term "construct" rather than "concept" in ethical discourse suggests that the method whereby decisions are made has confronted (a) the hard data drawn from the discipline or study to which the decision will refer; (b) the meeting of ontological polarities, i.e., the individual must meet the reality of the society through the personal while the society must not suppress the reality of the individual as personal. The operational perspective, then, contrary to strict Skinner behaviorism, creates a free-flowing interchange of data, ideas, and methods with the constructs it utilizes toward the process of decision-making. "To adopt the operational point of view . . . means a far-reaching change in all our habits of thought, in that we shall no longer permit ourselves to use as tools in our thinking concepts of which we cannot give an adequate account in terms of operations."[3] Approaching the problem negatively, we ask, does the construct one employs in ethical discussion, in the creation of norms, create more problems than it answers by being devoid of a content and form which allow it to function in a practical way?

In order to pursue a religious ethic based on an operational process, I will first describe the insufficiency of existing religious paradigms in longstanding need of reevaluation. The Judeo-Christian paradigms demythologized, liberalized and reformed, remain inadequate to the task of contemporary technocratic ethics. This thesis entails a reflective look at the nature of the "religious" which I contend is a far cry from the "spiritual" to which traditional paradigms usually refer. Second, a discussion of some examples of the problem of the individual as personal confronting rather than meeting the social, will show the inadequacy of traditional paradigms. Thirdly, I will suggest that the operational approach entailing a process of decision-making, utilizing the process of forming constructs, may be a way of reshaping the paradigms in the light of (a) the scientific study of religion, (b) the lack of biblical and/or spiritual precedents for the problems of a technocratic society, and (c) the need for self-identity which psychology, peripheral religious groups, and new sociological forms have expressed in this decade.

Paradigms are defined by Dr. Thomas Kuhn as "universally recognized scientific achievements that for a time provide model problems and solutions to a community of practitioners."[4] Whether it be in science or religion the definition is applicable. If one discards the word "scientific" one is faced with what experience would apply to "religion" in its traditional forms. I suggest that, while the word will vary with differing religious traditions, the word "moral" (in the Roman Catholic tradition, the word "dogma") would suffice to exemplify a historically acceptable concept which has been employed to provide model problems and responses for the communication of norms. However, these concepts are not necessarily constructs in the operational sense. In many instances they cannot be tested by exposing them to one or the other ontological polarity. One obvious area is birth control. Nevertheless, with a reconstructed religious truth, "religion" itself could be substituted for "scientific achievement."

In the area of birth control the quality of integrity within the Roman Catholic tradition has fallen considerably because the individual cannot test the practical aspect of this prohibition. The rightness or wrongness of the issue cannot be discussed because these aspects are lost amid the redefined construct "survival," which, because of its operational quality, is the favored option.[5] The same situation obtains when we concern ourselves with the question of abortion in all traditions and denominations. The duality of concerns, personal and social, do not lend themselves to easy solution. To allow a resolution of conflict, workable constructs must be developed on the basis of (1) available data, (2) reshaped religious paradigms, (3) present needs, (4) future projections.

Within the Christian persuasion—a multitheological persuasion —many *symbols of the "healing process" of Christianity spirituality* form the backdrop for decision-making in the matter of moral problems. Such symbols, reflecting the social implications of the Christian message, suggest the possible conceptual models which form the framework for normative moral principles, and are represented by (1) the creation, fall, redemption image of revelation; (2) the justification by faith image of soteriology; (3) the sanctification image of the Word of God; and (4) the discipleship image.[6] However, in view of what Professor Eugene Fontinell has called "the radical reconstruction of religious truth,"[7] traditional moral imperatives derived from these images simply serve to reinforce the repressed feeling of man rather than to satisfy his creative, personal, and social identity. Morality, as a set of norms derived from the religious tradition represented by each of the symbols of the healing process cited above, must be thrown back to the larger task of ethics itself. Following a relational perspective, Professor Fontinell describes the task of ethics in a modified operational form. Ethics is "a metaphysics of morality, that is, with an effort to ground, explain and defend the reasons or principles employed in the concrete act of making a moral decision."[8] Traditional paradigms and their pursuant modes of behavior, along with the moral relativism of the sixties (represented by the situationism of Joseph Fletcher)[9] require a cessation of polarization and a reflective look at ethical concerns on the basis of operational constructs. The reasoning behind this position comes from outside the realm of religion. The validity of moral concepts, as "constructs," must be tested in the practical spheres of living.

The societal model offers technology not merely as a passing fad but rather, as Jacques Ellul has suggested, as a system, a way of thinking, being, and acting characterized by mechanism, efficiency, autonomy, and self-augmentation.[10] Efficient operation with the

least amount of pain, guilt, and effort becomes the goal, and precision is virtue. Technique can be equal to the most profound
religious truth because it now operates in the personal areas of
medical issues, ecological concerns, psychological identity, mass
media. As Daniel Bell has also suggested, "Technology is not
simply a 'machine,' but a systematic, disciplined approach to
objectives, using a calculus of precision and measurement, and a
concept of system that are quite at variance with traditional and
customary religious, aesthetic and intuitive modes."[11] Yet, technique has a very positive side. It challenges the religious, aesthetic,
and intuitive modes to construct ways of responding to the complex intangibles on which technique thrives. Technique does not
eliminate the need for the multiple dimensions of human existence.
On the contrary, rather than destroying the possibility for "the
spiritual," "the beautiful," "the true," and "the good," as meaningful concepts, technique demands that we know precisely what
we are about when we try to define, limit, and prescribe the nature
of these intangibles. However, it does the same in the realm of
the ethical. Technique respects the qualities of movement, decision, independence, precision, and operation. It appears that a
more adequate meeting of the problem of technique within the
paradox of the individual meeting the social can be accomplished
within the parameters of those qualities through the careful
examination of the constructs used in ethical discourse and those
which motivate ethical behavior.

An example of operationalism in an area outside of the realm
of ethics is provided by Dr. Dolfman's approach to a model of
health.[12] "Health" becomes a working construct within the format
he suggests, comprising both the individual concern for health and
the social norms for establishing the principles of good health.
He considers the following factors—the kind of subjects, the
nature of the environment, the stimulus, the response of the sub-
ject(s) in the environment to the stimulus—and makes a correlation between these factors and the concepts fundamental to the
implications of health. He describes these implications as "functioning," "adapting," and "normal," and offers the following individual models:

An individual is healthy (that is, has attained or is in the state or condition known as health) if he is functioning adequately in a stated environment; and if while functioning in this environment he is subjected to some sort of stress, he is able to adapt to this stress within the range of normal functioning.

An individual is not healthy if he is not functioning adequately in a stated environment; or if while functioning in this environment, he is subjected to some sort of stress, he does not adapt within the normal range of functioning.[13]

What is more important than the models of the healthy and the unhealthy individuals themselves is the process by which these models are constructed. Dr. Dolfman describes the process which is analogous to the building of constructs from concepts, relations, and operations in physics, and analogous to what might be possible in religion and ethical discourse attendant to decision-making.

It is important to note that an operational model of health has been developed as opposed to an operational definition of health. It is felt that one would not have an operational definition until he knows what to count as "an environment," as "functioning," as a "stress," as "adapting," and as "normal." What has been done, however, is to take these key concepts and place them in a format, i.e., a model which contains the potential for allowing individuals and groups to generate their own operational definitions for health. In this task, these people are the ones who will have to specify the nature of the environment, what constitutes adequate functioning, the identity of the stress, and what constitutes normal adapting. The format can be likened to the logical analogy, x implies y. This form identifies a specific relationship which exists between two distinct entities. However, the entities themselves must be identified and/or defined before the relationship can have a distinct meaning. The operational model of health identifies the relationship which exists between those concepts which are fundamental to an understanding of the meaning of the word "health."[14]

The most important element in the format is the element of "specific relationship" which adds the element of the concrete to the process itself. No model or definition may be described as operational until it has a concrete focus.

This same precision may be asked when we describe, for example, the ethical value of moral codes, such as the Decalogue, the relational significance of the Beatitudes, the rediscovery of salvation in a time of parapsychology and transpersonal psychology, the reshaping of the concept "soul," and the definitions and/or descriptions of man's nature and God's being from Hindu pre-Aryan animism to liberal Christian and Jewish theology of the twentieth century. The precision of the behaviorism of B. F. Skinner leaves us without words when we come to decision-making in an age of technocracy.[15] Thus, it seems to me that the same kind of precision is possible in the area of the process of developing constructs to direct one's decision-making individually, personally, and socially. We need to review models such as the Commandments and the Beatitudes and concepts such as the soul and salvation to reshape them into workable constructs—if that is possible. If a correlation can be established between what they do and the data of experience to which they refer in the ethical realm, and if they can reflect other dimensions of man's existence without violating in a harmful way the academic and unavoidable truths of existence then such religious paradigms can serve as constructs in ethical discourse. If they cannot, then the source of ethical norms must be found in paradigms not drawn from religion as it is traditionally known.

The acknowledgment of the limitations of such a venture is most important.[16] Precision in ethics calls for a distinction between individual ethical and personal ethical responsibility and social responsibility, given the fact that "responsibility" means "ability to respond." Professor Niebuhr's problematic may be tested not only in the political arena, but also in the theoretical and practical ethical issues. Professor Dobzhansky, in his *Biological Basis of Human Freedom,* states: "Moral rightness and wrongness . . . have meaning only in connection with persons who are free agents, and who are consequently able to choose between different ideas and between possible courses of action. Ethics presupposes freedom."[17] But where does this freedom originate? Many dimensions of life point to conflicting aspects of freedom. Total license is virtually inoperable in our society. The economic, legal, and social boundaries make that impossible even though it appears as if that is not the case. From the sciences, we get a picture of freedom as the capacity to change, to select possibilities.[18]

> . . . We have seen that there are restrictions on such freedom imposed by nature, which decrees that most random choices are self-destructive. Hence, for living systems to evolve above rather primitive or unstable levels, freedom also comes to mean the *capacity* to make choices that are partially preadapted to the conditions which nature imposes. We have briefly touched upon some aspects of the evolution of new levels of choice-making systems that are less fully random and more homeostatic—from recombination of genes to association in brains. We have found that in biological evolution from primitive cells to men there is an increase in the range of adaptation and adaptability by making choices. This increase is based on accumulated genetic information about what is viable. We have also seen that in the evolution of the human brain, which makes possible greatly enhanced conscious selection, the patterns of choosing are guided by cultural as well as genetic information about self and surroundings. In human brains there has evolved the largest capacity of freedom to make viable choices that we know about. The evolution of religious and other cultural wisdom provides human brains with grounds for ever more advanced choices. The more detailed scientific information about what freedom means provides guidance for the further conscious enlargement of human freedom.[19]

In discerning the dimensions of one's existence in which one can exercise individually and socially a comfortable degree of freedom, within an acknowledged set of limitations, one can better proceed to the kind of certitude about one's field of operation demanded for decision-making. Freedom may then become a construct if in operation it satisfies the requirements of what constitutes a construct. Within the parameters of the individual, personal, and social categories three distinct operations must be analyzed. These operations, while relational, are distinct one from the other. An individual is a being in the world who at times, few and far between, really enjoys a sense of "being by himself." Economically, psychologically, and socially as well as culturally, he is dependent and as such not really isolated. For example, an individual exists within a legal structure, and as such is distinct from another individual, yet by relational bonds each individual tends toward the social.

The personal refers to the relational quality established between the social speaking to the individual. An individual may speak as a person but until he/she is acknowledged as such, the individual remains distinct and unrelated to others except by the contingencies of social structures like economics and the like. The social is also a given category. We live in societies. The social is more than a number of individuals. The relationship established between more than one individual may be personal (as a quality of individuality), or simply technological. However, the social as communal (exceeding two in number) is an idealized concept which may not be applicable to the construct of freedom at all. Freedom may not be operable in the context of social, i.e., communal, limitations to the personal quality of relationship. On the other hand, society may prove to be most conducive to the constructive use of freedom. Experience is there to tell. However, the labeling a priori of certain ways of being as automatically free without the benefit of environmental analysis or a study of the entities abstractly (and hypothetically) removed from the natural environment may only prove to create more problems than the concept attempted to answer. Freedom is not a good. Freedom experienced in a situation between two individuals who have established a personal quality through relationship is a good.

It is also within the reshaped construct "freedom" that we discover the basic limitation to doing ethics in general. Individual ethics and personal ethics and social ethics are distinct avenues of concern. The establishment of the meeting of these avenues is what the construct and its testable operation are all about. I will offer some examples illustrative of the problem of moral positions which are devoid of considerations of the distinctly different operations of the individual, the personal, and the social, and indicate the need to go outside the field of the abstract concept of freedom in order to develop a position which is operative for our concern.

The first example is taken from Reinhold Niebuhr's examination of the relation of the individual man in a collective (group) to religion and morality. In his statement of the ethical paradox he reflects the problematic of the limitation to freedom as imposed by "the brutal character of the behavior of all human collectives."[20] The freedom of the individual—even with the highest spiritual motives, expressed by the desire to be absorbed by the infinite—is stubbornly resisted by the "power of the whole." What then is the relationship between the personal and the social if this position of Professor Niebuhr's is held? Although he maintains that two distinct ethics must be maintained each ruled by opposite principles at times, I believe that this polarization can be bridged by a construct such as freedom, which would be used only in a context in which the following obtains: the relevant data is considered (environment, possibilities, limitations), value is created, and violent compromises of interest on one side or the other are not made. Unless the construct "freedom" is used in this way, freedom is a meaningless cliché and Henri Bergson's observation is correct—we have few true moments of freedom.

Some examples of ethical problems offer vivid illustrations of the conflict between individual decision-making and social behavior in the realm of the possibilities and limitations to freedom. The first may be found in an examination of the problematic of the Supreme Court decision regarding abortion.[21] While freeing the individual to a socially viable alternative the decision does nothing to speak to the dimensions of an individual's life relating to personal meaning, intention, and goals. In this context new social possibility creates a limit by forcing the individual to bear the burden of decision-making without the method whereby what is possible becomes personal in a "yes" or "no" response of value to the now legally acceptable alternative (within the limit of the first three months of pregnancy). Further, a conflict between the ultimate religious values and the legal values established by the moral authority of the nation is inevitable.

A poignant sample of the conflict in the area of the personal quality of moral principles is found in a critical study done by a team of medical and religious professionals from the University of California, San Diego. This study, "Birth Control, Sterilization and Abortion: Attitudes of Catholic and Protestant Clergymen in San Diego toward Use in Families with Genetic Illness,"[22] reveals that religious traditions avoid the social and medical meeting of their traditions with biomedical technocratic discoveries. While

Catholic and Protestant clergymen follow one image or symbol of healing process or another, their responses to the questionnaire indicate that they *do not* consider such factors as severity of genetic illness, or the socio-ethnic factors, in making a decision. Rather, religious beliefs were the determinants of their decisions. (I would offer that the same situation obtains in the pro-life as well as pro-abortion positions.) A priori, or cultural, values provide the rationale for decision rather than a well-thought-out process utilizing constructs. The concluding remark of the study states:

> . . . Since they [clergymen] are so intimately involved in health care it would seem essential that, in the case of genetic illness particularly, more studies and more discussion should take place between health care providers and the clergy.[23]

This evidence quite forcefully shows the need for the adoption within the San Diego area of the theoretical and practical structures of institutes or centers for the exchange of information, ideas, and multidimensional approaches to the problems of biomedical concern such as birth control and the question of human experimentation. (Institutes such as the Kennedy Center for Bioethics, Washington, D.C., the Institute of Society, Ethics, and the Life Sciences, Hastings-on-Hudson, New York, as well as the Institute of Religion and Human Development, Texas Medical Center, Houston, are engaged in the interdisciplinary approach to information which is disseminated by researcher to doctor, priest, minister, rabbi, and in turn, by those whose thinking is altered by this shared framework.) Further, the study demonstrates that these individuals lack the ability to respond intelligently to radical changes in the nature of the new ethics. A similar study has been done with regard to predicting voting behavior in abortion reform legislation on the basis of religious affiliation (Mormon, Catholic, Protestant).[24] Although done in 1969, it shows significantly that predictability of religious loyalty has not changed notably in spite of vastly enhanced knowledge.[25]

A study of attitudes toward abortion among nurses and social workers indicates that religion (defined as church attendance) among conservatives and liberals, more than other variables, influenced the disapproval of abortion.[26] Religious paradigms and goals are accepted without reflective questioning of their relation to the subject at hand. When religion blocks the search for answers to vital questions without knowledge of what technical science is about, i.e., without the proper constructs for a response of value, it is acting irresponsibly. I concur with Hans Jonas who has stated it this way:

> . . . It will be my contention that with certain developments of our powers the nature of human action has changed, and since ethics is concerned with action, it should follow that the changed nature of human action calls for a change in ethics as well; this not merely in the sense that new objects of action have added to the case material on which received rules of conduct are to be applied, but in the more radical sense that the qualitatively novel nature of certain of our actions has opened a whole new dimension of ethical relevance for which there is no precedent in the standards and canons of traditional ethics.[27]

Religion in its traditional forms alone cannot give the ability to respond. The paradox of individual, personal, and social ethical conflict calls for a reconstruction of religious truth through (1) a restructuring and firming up of the parameters of its concern, i.e., a separation of the spiritual from the religious (ethical); (2) a redefinition of the place of pertinent disciplines, such as medicine, psychology, law, and sociology, in the restructuring of the parameters; (3) an immanent rather than a totally transcendent or "supernatural" approach to the nature of the divine; (4) a recognition of individual ethics, personal ethics, *and* social ethics as separate, joined only by meaningful constructs which operate by meeting the paradox itself. In this regard scientists themselves are relating to the process within the nature of the material forms of life to discern the relevance of the qualitative dimension of life which we call "the religious." A leading professor of psychobiology at the California Institute of Technology, Dr. Roger W. Sperry opts for "a science of values" resulting from "a fusion of sciences, ethics and religion that would bring the insight, knowledge and principles of science to bear upon the whole problem of values and value priorities."[28] Many mistrust science because they blame science for technological mayhem. However, "what has failed is not science but rather the value and belief systems of man that have determined the way in which his scientific advances have been applied."[29] Certain invalid postulates and ultimate goals permeate our way of thinking and prevent the positive value of science from aiding us.

> Instead of relation to a single omnipotent personal control force, man would relate to a vast complex of forces, hierarchically interlocked from the subatom through the cellular, organismic, social and even galactic levels in a great pluralistic system of controls all differentiated from, and united in, a common foundation.
>
> . . . The "grand design of nature" as seen through the expanding eyes of modern science would appear already in its present form to contain as much to sustain the highest in man's religious and spiritual experience as do some of the comparatively simple metaphysical schemes that have had wide acceptance. A scientific approach would not lead to a rigid, closed scheme, but rather to one that would continue to unfold and enlarge indefinitely as science and understanding advance.[30]

Operating under a relational position, the construct "grand design of nature" becomes not an idealized hierarchical scheme but an active, immanent process which takes its meaning from what nature is doing and not from what we think nature ought to do.[31]

Professor Charles Birch, senior lecturer in zoology at the University of Sidney, suggests that the process of nature, interpreted from the higher to the lower, implies a meaning.[32] Professor Birch qualifies his ethical position in terms of *integrity,* i.e., undivided, at-one-ment, wholeness, health, and holiness.[33]

The qualitative dimension of life can then unite the facets of existence which require various normative and descriptive guides. For many charismatic thinkers of our time such as Alfred North Whitehead and Pierre Teilhard de Chardin, unity exists only in diversity. Diversity represents the concrete particular decisions in the process itself; unity represents the importance attached to the issues and concerns demanding reflective, responsible (i.e., the ability to respond) behavior.

The restructuring of our parameters also requires psychological insight into the nature of man—for soul, salvation, integrity, *psyche, anima,* all are relational. They construct a self-centeredness, a focus of "I." The place of the emotions, the hopes, the fears, the anxieties of life contribute both to the total picture of what exactly is a free response. Morality assumes man is "rational" and "mature" enough to recognize his misdeeds and misactions especially when he has the spiritual guidance of what Paul Tillich, a philosophical theologian, calls "the wisdom of the ages," such as the Ten Commandments and the Beatitudes. Unfortunately, wisdom must be reflected upon by the self who is caught in the very paradox being discussed. A vicious circle must therefore be broken by a radical intrusion of man as the one who "truths," thereby making the valuable visible and immoral. For example, "To speak of man as a soul is, then, to speak mythologically, but in a way which is bound up with important practical attitudes and practices. The myth of the soul expresses a faith in the intrinsic value of the human individual as an end in himself."[34] This does not imply a negation of dimensions other than the human but it does stress that "soul-language as a valuation of mankind" is the product of the same evolutionizing process as that by which we define bodily and material development.

The question of survival is an ethical concern—not so much a question of what but a question of how. I have suggested that, instead of pulling abstract paradigms from the past, we develop operable constructs from a combination of paradigms in relation to present resources The reshaping of religion must also suggest the relocation of religion in ethics. Piety, community, and inward renewal have a most important place in one dimension of life— the spiritual—but that is quite different from the quality of personal *value* with which religion is concerned in the technocratic puzzle of individual and social decision-making. The religious problematic demands a restructuring of epistemological parameters which involve the paradoxical unity of limit and possibility and directly relating to the perspective of that which binds together the intimate complex of man, the divine (as operable) and nature toward the concern of bioethics and abortion. Perhaps, however, some would be more comfortable if I did elaborate the distinction between the "spiritual" and the "religious."

From the perspective of the ethical paradox I have maintained that it is most difficult to take man out of his environment—in fact it is impossible since environment may be broadly described to mean those conditions to which we conform presently. It could be equally well argued that a multidimensional approach to that environment including the psychological motivations and the actual behaviors of men is necessary. A multidimensional approach could include distinct areas of man's well-being and exclude none presently known to explain, describe, or aid man. It could further describe in operational terms the basic content of the dimensions which I have called the "spiritual" and the "religious." The spiritual dimension may coexist with the religious dimension. However, neither exists by itself and both may overlap the domain of the other to a certain extent. I would maintain that the life of piety and prayer are specifically derived from either a religious tradition as that is commonly understood, for example, Christianity, Buddhism, Judaism, or from an immanent/transcendent experience derived from one of the phenomena characterized as the "'new religions" of the sixties and seventies. Usually an a priori assumption precedes the acceptance of the experience, either traditional or "new." That a priori assumption may be a traditional, dialectical religious language, or a strict empirical basis for accepting the importance of transcendence itself. However, spirituality forms the inner movement of man-in-culture. Spirituality becomes the domain of the personal apprehension and appreciation of what the faith commitment contains and from which it operates. As such, the spiritual function of man usually proceeds from a content which is scriptually and divinely oriented, whether the individual be of the contemporary Christian free-thinking fundamentalist type or of the old order denominational type. The minister of the spiritual serves a distinct function. He serves the commitment of the dialectic to which the assumptions regarding faith refer. This is not the wisdom referred to earlier in the chapter. Wisdom has to do with values and the valuative process, i.e., making valuable. In order to make some thing or event of value, its content may reveal a novel approach to the nature of the content itself. It may ask for a reshaping of the existing order of priorities in order to accommodate the demands of unprecedented appeal. Such is the case in the discipline of bioethics, as well as in the areas of the crises in conscience-authority relationship recently presented by the My Lai massacre and the Watergate affront.

In many ways the reshaping of existing paradigms, as well as the restructuring of our epistemological parameters, may demand that we go outside of the faith commitment, as has been the case for so many in the Roman Catholic theological circle. Professional judgment has caused a personal faith crisis. The result is that many times religion as an operative phenomenon is lost socially and, eventually, personally and individually. Religion, however, may be precisely the area of the ethician's dimension. It may be up to the ethician to be aware of the reshaped definitions of religion itself and to promote a generalized description of the phenomena which ask the ultimately serious questions of our life—past, present, and future.[35] Theology is limited by its specific concern with God-language in a particular faith context; spirituality is convinced of the faith commitment and, therefore, cannot enter the realm of the unprecedented, although it may be the cause of transcendent, personal experience; religion can seek within and without the realms of experience, including the past moral and ethical directions and not excluding the sciences of our century and the information which we have gleaned from them. The only responsibility religion has is to promote a "response of lasting value." For this reason we must explore the parameters of this process of the religious. Also, we must press the issue of the importance of the valuable by referring to the thought of Alfred North White-head whose psychological and ethical approach to decision-making increases our awareness of the necessity of a distinct realm of the ethical that is religious. The emerging ethician employs the Heisenberg Principle of Uncertainty or Indeterminancy: no matter what variable is known and to what extent, the other variable will always create only the possible and never the predictable.[36] Because of this canopy of a novel and, for this present

29

time at least, natural law (derived from modern physics) the ethician as religious must live in the state of uncertainty with only this "natural" principle as his a priori assumption.

NOTES

1. Kenneth Vaux, *Biomedical Ethics: Morality for the New Medicine* (New York: Harper & Row, 1974), p. xvi.
2. P. W. Bridgman, *The Logic of Modern Physics* (New York: Macmillan, 1927), pp. 53, 55–56.
3. Ibid., p. 31; cf. P. W. Bridgman, *The Intelligent Individual and Society* (New York: Macmillan, 1938), p. 20. Operational analysis is described as what one is *doing* in using a term or answering a question. Sir Arthur Eddington also adopts an operational perspective. See *The Mathematical Theory of Relativity* (London: Cambridge University Press, 1924).
4. Thomas S. Kuhn, *The Structure of Scientific Revolutions*, 2d ed., enlarged (Chicago: University of Chicago Press, 1972), p. viii. This work is part of the series, International Encyclopedia of Unified Science, vol. II, no. 2.
5. Cf. Daniel Callahan, *The Tyranny of Survival and Other Pathologies of Civilized Life* (New York: Macmillan, 1973).
6. James F. Smurl, *Religious Ethics: A Systems Approach* (Englewood Cliffs, N.J.: Prentice-Hall, 1972), pp. 54 ff.
7. Eugene Fontinell, "Religious Truth in a Relational and Processive World," *Cross Currents* XVII, no. 3 (Summer 1967), pp. 283 ff.
8. Eugene Fontinell, "Towards an Ethics of Relationship," in *Situationism and the New Morality*, ed. R. L. Cunningham (New York: Appleton-Century-Crofts, 1970), p. 199.
9. Cf. Joseph Fletcher, *Moral Responsibility* (Philadelphia: Westminster Press, 1967); *Morals and Medicine* (Boston: Beacon Press, 1954); *Situation Ethics* (Philadelphia: Westminster Press, 1966); *The Ethics of Genetic Controls: Ending Reproductive Roulette* (Garden City: Doubleday Anchor, 1974).
10. Cf. Jacques Ellul, *The Technological Society* (New York: Random House, Vintage Books, 1964).
11. Daniel Bell, "The Trajectory of an Idea," *Daedalus*, vol. 96, no. 3 (Summer 1967), p. 643.
12. Cf. Michael L. Dolfman, "Toward Operational Definitions of Health," *Journal of School Health* XLIV, no. 4 (April 1974), pp. 206–209.
13. Ibid., p. 207.
14. Ibid.
15. Cf. B. F. Skinner, *Walden II* (New York: Macmillan, 1960); *Beyond Freedom and Dignity* (New York: Knopf, 1971).
16. Cf. Bridgman, Logic of Modern Physics, chap. I, "Broad Points of View."

17. Cf. Theodosius Dobzhansky, *Biological Basis of Human Freedom,* quoted in *Man: The New Humanism,* ed. Roger L. Shinn, introduction by W. Hordern, series: *New Directions in Theology Today,* vol. VI (Philadelphia: Westminster Press, 1968), p. 86.

18. Alfred F. Emerson and Ralph Wendell Burhoe, "Evolutionary Aspects of Freedom, Death, and Dignity," *Zygon* IX, no. 2 (June 1974), p. 167.

19. Ibid.

20. Cf. Introduction, note 23.

21. See Decision of the United States Supreme Court, January 22, 1972.

22. J. J. Schneiderman, M.D.; Lorraine Prichard, P.H.N.; Scott Fuller, M.A.; and Leslie Atkinson, B.D., M.A., "Birth Control, Sterilization and Abortion: Attitudes of Catholic and Protestant Clergymen in San Diego toward Use in Families with Genetic Illness," *Western Journal of Medicine* CXX, no. 2 (February 1974), pp. 174–179.

23. Ibid., p. 179.

24. James T. Richardson and Sandie Wightman Fox, "Religious Affiliation as a Predictor of Voting Behavior in Abortion Reform Legislation," *Journal of the Scientific Study of Religion XI* (December 1972), pp. 347–359. Abstract:

> In this research, religious affiliation is taken as an independent variable and an examination is made of the voting behavior on abortion reform legislation of members of two sessions of the state legislature of a western state which has large groups of Catholics, Mormons, and Protestants—religious groups with differences on the abortion issue. As expected, knowledge of the religious affiliation of the legislators allows better prediction of such voting behavior than constituency, party, or age, and controlling for these three variables affects the size of the association only slightly and occasionally. The effect of the religious affiliation variable is particularly dramatized in the shift of Mormon lower house members' votes from 1967 to 1969, a time period during which the Mormon Church made official statements against abortion reform legislation. Ramifications and alternative explanations of the data are presented. (p. 347)

One of the primary concerns of those reflecting on the legislation was for the "soul of the individual who is kept from earthly existence (and therefore future heavenly existence) by the abortion" (p. 351).

25. An interesting study of religion among intellectuals was done by Gordon F. De Jong and Joseph E. Faulkner, "Religion and the Intellectuals: Findings from a Sample of University Faculty," *Review of Religious Research* XIV, no. 1 (Fall 1972), pp. 15–24. Abstract:

> In-depth interviews averaging two and one-half hours with a sample of 56 university faculty suggest that intellectuals are not divorced from involvement in the religious life. Few could be characterized as totally rejecting traditional aspects of religion and thus fulfilling the stereotype of the "atheistic" professor. However, when assessed against the tenets of the Apostles' Creed, there is a marked departure from these orthodox Christian beliefs. Although deviating from traditional beliefs, over half of the respondents belong to a church, attend services fairly regularly, and consider church membership and prayer to be important in their lives. *A large majority also report that Biblical teachings exert an indirect influence on*

31

everyday decision-making. What emerges is a picture of *intellectuals who have rather thoroughly demythologized the core beliefs of the Christian faith but, nevertheless, continue to practice their faith in both individual and institutional contexts.* [emphasis mine]

The study further indicated an ambiguity concerning the future of the church in society: 38% favor more social action; 27% the maintenance of traditional functions, i.e., preach the gospel (spiritual functions in my discourse); 17% to move toward ecumenical emphasis; 9% emphasized the improvement of individuals. Within the 38%, two different responses were noted: 1) "The church must develop a wide area of agreement on a set of social ethics that can easily be applied to a number of different social problems that we confront; . . . the question of what is right or wrong . . . will probably always have to be debated, but the task would be easier if the churches were to place more emphasis on the social implications of the New Testament gospel." 2) ". . . the church has been too inactive in political affairs on a world scale. Merely getting to believe in a supreme being will not solve the world's problems." (p. 22)

26. Bradley Hertel, Gerry E. Hendershot, James W. Grimm, "Religion and Attitudes toward Abortion: A Study of Nurses and Social Workers," *Journal for the Scientific Study of Religion* XIII, no. 1 (March 1974), pp. 23–34

27. Hans Jonas, "Technology and Responsibility: Reflections on the New Task of Ethics," in *Religion and the Humanizing of Man*, ed. James M. Robinson (Waterloo, Ontario: Council on the Study of Religion, 1972), p. 1.

28. R. W. Sperry, "Science and the Problem of Values," *Zygon* IX, no. 1 (March 1974), p. 11.

29. Ibid. p. 13.

30. Ibid., p. 20.

31. Ibid.; cf. p. 16: "A thing or concept is perceived and gets meaning and value only in terms of a background, a surround, something beyond or different from itself."

32. Cf. Charles Birch, "Interpreting the Lower in Terms of the Higher," Process Studies Center Reprint, originally published in *The Christian Scholar*, reprinted by the Center for Process Studies.

33. Cf. Charles Birch, "Purpose in the Universe: A Search for Wholeness," *Zygon* VI, no. 1 (March 1971), p. 5.

34. John Hick, *Biology and the Soul* (London: Cambridge University Press, 1972), p. 23.

35. Cf. Paul Tillich, *Biblical Religion and the Search for Ultimate Reality,* (Chicago: University of Chicago Press, 1965 [1955]).

36. Cf. Ian G. Barbour, *Issues in Science and Religion* (New York: Harper & Row, Harper Torchbooks, 1971, originally published by Prentice-Hall, Englewood Cliffs, N.J.), pp. 279–282.

II

"Religion" in Need
of Restructured
Epistemological Parameters

The reshaping of the religious toward the concrete ethical concerns of our technocracy requires educational rehabilitation. Educational rehabilitation involves learning to outline "constructs" and reshape paradigms to establish the epistemological parameters of decision-making. This would involve learning to utilize a phenomenology of imagination to create dynamic fields of operability for the existing religious ethical needs to be "self-possessed" as well as "self-authenticated" by others. Man as an individual and as a social being is a paradox of conflicting needs and values. Man is productive of the "valuable." This productivity threatens existing "institutionalism" which is founded on the permanence rather than the flexibility of values. Man, therefore, must operate within "lived truth." Educational rehabilitation involves a "value ontology," a structure (characterized by its integrative "response" quality) in which values are acknowledged as satisfying the above needs in and through being. Values are found in the possibilities and limitations of the individual in the everyday social "field" in which the "I" functions. A teleological "response of value" directs (within the process of discovery) the human quest for the "valuable." Unless this quest is openly acknowledged as necessary to the demands of our present life, the mediocre and purely relevant will be our operational standards.

"Value ontology" may be described as a method of viewing man and his milieu as a field of operability in which that operability is conditioned by contrasts, alternatives, psychosocial and environmental limitations, and possibilities known only in a particular response of value to particular impression, concept, feeling, perception, persons or objects in the "lived concrete."[1] As such it is also a construct proceeding from an operational, process philosophy. The "valuable" is the priority made by the deliberate choice on the part of man in the process of discovering his authentic existence through a complex culture which includes a holistically economic measure of man's achievements. For example, in the issue of abortion, the paradox of man's individual existence against the quality of his life-stance is resolved only as decision-making gives the issue an "ontological status." Personally, abortion may be repugnant to the individual for religious or psychological reasons. Socially, this same individual may accept and encourage the "ontological status" of the matter by accepting the right of abortion of those who freely and seriously choose it. Thus, the problematic of abortion, by means of the processive nature of man's decision-making power, and, by his ability to see alternatives within a plurality of needs, has moved from a question of mere existence to a question of the quality of life, in other words, to the issue of the valuable.

What I am concerned with is a basic "functional wisdom" which must be the foundation of religious ethical constructs. Operational, or functional, wisdom assumes the character of a philosophic canopy to the present condition of man as he is defined in a world of operations and movements. In the midst of political and social upheaval, religion in its varied forms and expressions is a dynamic field—value ontology—through which and about which individuals and social structures do function directly or indirectly. Only by reflecting on this "dynamic field" can religion be described as "meaning and motivation in action systems."

A response of value is built upon the "educational rehabilitation" of religious man as a self and as a member of numerous societal structures destroying and creating values in the twentieth century. Thus, for a time, religion so defined has been sublimated and superceded by ethics. Educational rehabilitation involves the assertion of such disciplines as theology, philosophy, psychology, sociology, and anthropology in the meeting of the finite moral codes and norms arising out of theological traditions.[2] The religious education of man must begin at the door of the relation of man to himself, to others, and to the institutions which seem to control his life. The adequacy or inadequacy of these relationships must be a guide to the reconstruction of man for they tell man why he is who he is. They provide the historical, experimental, and ontological character of man's meaning. It is within this character of man in his environment—past, present, and future—that the "valuable" will be found.[3] As such the "valuable" will be the transcendent quality of man's experience. If the "valuable" is a functioning vehicle for a permanent "issue" it will be called a value. The "valuable," then, is the priority made by the deliberate choice on the part of man in the process of discovering his authentic existence through a complex culture. What is or will be valuable cannot be determined a priori for then we would be destroying the character of man in his societal relationships to evaluate for himself, or, if he so chooses, to let others value for him. Thus, educational rehabilitation means the discovery of the meaningful authenticity of man through the response of value in a necessarily ontological structure which is organic to his life.[4]

Five aspects of this life of the quest for the "valuable" are most important to man: (1) the memory of man, (2) the power of forgetfulness, (3) the use of the imagination including (a) the importance of intensity which he attaches to his particular concern and (b) the ability to *transcend* the particularity of his past and present to a concern for the future. (The future can only be expressed as concern because it is unknown and is based on the idealized wholeness of man in the present.)

In order to begin this process of rehabilitation the bewildered man of the changing religious ethical scene must be aware that he has a living, corporate memory by which he recalls the past and maintains an identity through present searching.[5] Man's memory is the unconscious and conscious collective value of the images of his past which have influenced his present on various levels of his functioning self. The memory of man has symbolic representations developed from actual physical and historical environmental conditions. Illustrating the physical source of a symbolic representation of man's memory, I will cite the paradoxical operation of the genetic code itself. While the chromosomal structure of DNA and RNA can be mapped out developmentally, the unique character of the individual who is the product of this development cannot be charted after the master plan. That we can replicate the organismic model of the source of heredity is distinctly different from claiming that the governance of this model by a directional control (cybernetics) will remove the inner tendency to disorder, disturbance, and breakdown. Professor Ralph Wendell Burhoe cites replication and cybernation as the two basic characteristics of physical systems which contribute to the "prophecy of human values," yet he also admits that this predictive precision is useless without the environment—in this case, all protoplasm—to interpret it.[6] Further, by itself the DNA is merely an indicator of *possible combination patterns.* "The order, organizations, or meaningful design of the arrangement of a portion of a string of DNA, let us say a million DNA long, is just about as rare and improbable as your finding a million-letter sequence of the Bible or a scientific text coming out of a shaking hopper containing a million letters that were allowed to drop in a moneybelt."[7] While maintenance of living systems (homeostasis) is natural to those systems, the paradoxical chemistry value of "knowledge and ignorance" leaves the religiously oriented ethician in the dark regarding how much importance to place on the predictions of the world of science.

A further example of the symbolic representation through memory lies in the paradoxical relationship between history and political action. According to Johannes B. Metz, the *modus vivendi* for the operation of historical, political progress is precisely that which societies seek to alleviate—suffering. " . . . It is suffering that opposes an affirmative theory of reconciliation between man and nature. Every such attempt at simulation degenerates finally into the worst kind of ontologizing of man's torment. Suffering brings out the contrast between nature and history, between teleology and eschatology. There is no 'objective' reconciliation of the two, no transparent and manageable unity between them."[8] In discussing the function of memory as "practical-cultural, yes, ever dangerously liberating power," Professor Metz distinguishes kinds of memories and grounds his thesis in the Christian *memoria passionis* as an eschatological hope in response to the paradox of societal development through political interchange.[9] While I do not see the need to emphasize the Christian symbol of creative suffering, I do acknowledge that existential suffering motivates us to create new forms of response. In the Buddhist construct, "desire," or "thirst" (*dukkha*), the impetus as well as the limit of technology, science, and normative ethics in their expanded parameters is implied. Thus, in Metz's rationale, memory is activated by the symbolic form of a transcendent value as well as by physical facts and realities.

In the area of the reconstruction of values, or "truthing" as I call it, a revitalization of terms gives rise to a transcendent form of memory. The imaginative process of operational description provides the defining characteristics of an event, concept, or story so basic to the scrutiny of ethical evaluation. Further, this enables religion to move from traditional, denominational roles to psychosocial areas, to economic and political issues, to biomedical concerns, in a word to *ethics*. This occurs when memory is operating to indicate the various images and dimensions of reality functioning through symbolic representation prompted by variable conditions. The relationship between science and religion in the West is a primary example. The cosmic model led into the religious model which dictated how far the cosmic model could go. The circle was only broken by one who dared to challenge the existing model—whether it be Copernicus, Galileo, Darwin, or Einstein; of course, in the case of the first two the price was much greater. This manipulation of religion by science and vice versa has been confronted by a function of transcendent memory in the form of reflection on the process itself.

As suggested in the Introduction,[10] Professor Thomas Kuhn paved the way, through the use of the term "paradigm," for a subjective yet processive and relational explanation of the development of any model by which we imagine the cosmos. He endeavored to uncover the role of paradigms in scientific research. Paradigms form structural and working tools for the meeting of science and religion.

The maintenance of a continuity between religion and science motivated Professor Ian Barbour in *Science and Secularity* to reconstruct much of the traditional symbolic forms of religious language and imagery.[11] He also suggests relativity and novelty as conceptually characteristic of the *models* of religious vision, but he finds continuity as more characteristic.[12] He further finds that there are criteria common to all paradigms.[13] In his latest work, *Myths, Models and Paradigms*, Professor Barbour uses the term paradigm to refer to "a tradition transmitted through historical exemplars."[14] He defines a model as "a symbolic representation of selected aspects of the behavior of a complex system for particular purposes. It is an imaginative tool for ordering experience, rather than a description of the world."[15] His definition closely corresponds to Professor Kuhn's definition of paradigm. Through the combination of the basic paradigm, such as the Christian experience, and the attendant models which are possible, Professor Barbour develops the epistemological parameter of memory within the special function of the religious.

Ray L. Hart's description of a paradigm draws attention to the lack of continuity among paradigms. Paradigm literally means "to show forth pattern."[16] Paradigms are subsequent to the interconnection of an image of an event and an event itself. For events themselves do not occur in serial form but collect here and there like quanta. A paradigmatic event, therefore, is episodic, i.e., it has an initial and terminal situation, and is ambiguous in meaning.[17] He cites the Sinai Covenant as an example.

> This event doubtless had an initial situation, since the event itself calls all preceding events in the Exodus into focus. But should the initial situation be called altogether fixed, when whatever is fixed can only be understood through the master images of preceding history? The matter is circular and therefore ambiguous. From Egypt to Sinai is a course made intelligible by the event of Covenant: preceding events are thus co-ordinated by paradigmatic occurrence that is simultaneously event and image. No less surely, this occurrence had a terminal situation, else it would not have been an integral episode in the history of a people, a center for enucleating their self-images. Yet, that

terminal situation, however ontic in history, established a fund of ontological potency out of which succeeding generations were to live in one mode or another of appropriation. The paradigmatic event, we have said, is the event that keeps on happening: its terminal situation is open.[18]

Paradigms are seemingly clarified by tradition and history as well as by the frequency of their celebration. Paradigmatic events further serve to periodize time. "If the paradigmatic event is re-enacted and brought forward in public rite, that owes to the conviction that the event embodied in itself a co-inherence of the modes of time, and thus is the key to the temporal unity of history in which its celebrants stand."[19] They lead to articulated forms of their vitality; i.e., "systematic symbolics." It is necessary, therefore, to stress the subjective, cognitive, and feeling values— importance—of the one or group who takes an image arising from an event and articulate and communicate the process of "truthing" which has taken place. In this context myths and models become very important. For the most part models are the bases for knowing the historical paradigm in a particular context and time period.[20]

The concept "paradigm" presents itself as a functional, flexible, articulated symbol of transcendent memory. Within the framework of *ethics*, a "reshaping" (my term) of the paradigms verbally describes the function of ethics itself, i.e., a calling into question the established norms, once formed by images and events, and reshaped to fit the field of operation. Paradigms become "constructs" in an operational hypothesis of memory as an epistemological parameter.

Memory makes us conscious of the intimate reciprocity of men and values in historically cultural contexts. It gives us an evolved past, an active present, and an evolving, directional future. This direction is the "subjective aim" of which Whitehead speaks and permeates the quest for values which are the correlates to knowledge and to the impulse to action. Paraphrasing Bernard Lonergan, S.J., I would say the primary need for the philosopher of religion (or ethician) is to direct what he is doing when he is doing religious ethics.[21] He must direct it by connecting thought and action in value and by seeing value as part of a total organic function of human wisdom. In his cognitive approach Lonergan states:

> Man's development is a matter of getting beyond himself, of transcending himself, of ceasing to be an animal in a habitat and of becoming a genuine person in a community. The first stage of this development lies in the sensibility that enables him to perceive but also wonders, inquires, seeks to understand. He unifies and relates, constructs and extrapolates, serializes and generalizes. He moves out of his immediate surroundings into a universe put together by the symbols and stories of mythic consciousness, or by the speculations of philosophers, or by the investigations of scientists. But besides such cognitional self-transcendence, there is also a real self-transcendence. Men ask not only about facts but also about values. They are not content with satisfaction. They distinguish between what truly is good and what only apparently is good. They are stopped by the question: is what I have achieved really worthwhile? Is what I hope for worthwhile? Because men can raise such questions, and answer them, and live by the answers, they can be principles of benevolence and beneficence, of genuine cooperation, of true love.[22]

The above approach, however, is static, nonrelational, and nonoperative unless we have a method for cognitional self-transcendence. Only then will a real self-transcendence occur. What Lonergan misses is the fact that perception and cognition, valuing, transcending, etc., take place in an ontological setting and in a physical environment in which the facts of other ideas, persons, and pressures become occasions for the response of what is worthwhile or valuable. Lonergan offers an image of man as a cognitive being capable of self-transcendence in that process, when in experience man functions less as a cognitive being than as an imaginative projector of the phenomenal world. Michael Novak, gleaning his position on the subjective experience from Thomas S. Kuhn, Peter L. Berger, Thomas Luckmann, and Alfred Schutz, closely describes the "imaginative projection" alluded to above.[23] He uses the construct "standpoint." A standpoint is a complex of experiences, images, expectations, presuppositions, and operations (especially of inquiring and deciding) by which men act out their own sense of themselves, of others, of nature, of history, and of

God. A standpoint may be unthematized or thematized: operating unself-consciously, even unconsciously; or else brought to articulate awareness.[24] Professor Novak describes the six stages of his "system of coiling strands": experience, imagination, insight, method, self-criticism, and action.[25] All of these activities proceed from a self-image and projection *through* the self-image of the phenomenal world. Thus the subjectivity of the subject is most crucial to the process of grasping the paradigm he holds as valuable. What I am saying is that man grasps the symbolic representation of the past that he wants. He holds on to, and reshapes what he needs. Religion as an economic commodity doesn't cause men to behave any differently.[26] It, too, is based on the law of supply and demand. Yet, there is no method to this justification. While it may be true, it is not helpful for the religiously oriented ethician to begin to know what forms, verbal and historical, he may keep and what forms he may discard. If we understand the limit of the paradigms themselves and the function which we are asking constructs to perform we would then be able to ask how realistic those requests are in the light of (a) what *can* be done, (2) what we imagine, or require, or project, needs to be done.

The second aspect of educational rehabilitation is that of forgetfulness. In the same sense that man is a "living memory" (to us Augustine's term but not his meaning)),[27] man is also a forgetting being, the *yang* and the *yin* of his healthy survival. An example of the need for the process of forgetfulness involves the work of psychotherapy—individual and group psychotherapy. Through psychotherapy man can learn the process of reshaping the paradigms significant of one's life events and deal with the dangerous memories destructive to the full human being. This does not mean that one sublimates one's past, but it does mean that under the environment of free thought, word and action, the realization of memories and the dealing with them can efficiently take place. Then the parameters of "self-in-the-world" can be restructured to open new limits and possibilities of the present and the future.

The quality of forgetting is rare, but it is not to be confused with a refusal to face facts; for example, a refusal to face death

41

and its stark reality. It does not mean to dismiss concepts from our thoughts. It does mean to raise them to a level of consciousness so that they will dismiss themselves from being a preoccupation or something to run away from or to avoid. But to reshape the paradigm of death one must be willing to undergo the process of remembering, forgetting, and imaginatively creating through a reshaping of the paradigm and the employment of constructs suited to the teleological direction of this time. Even the ability to understand the language of contemporary ethical constructs, such as revealed in the following statement by Professor Moltmann, reflects the need for a recession of traditionally defined roles for such terms as "right to life," "right to death," and "art."

> An ethic of accepted, loved and experienced life must, for its part, practice attitudes toward death and liberate dying from its repression or glamorization. As life and love are an art, the ability to die is also an art. We indeed know, in the double sense, how one can "take life" but we know very little about how one can leave it humanly and with dignity.[28]

The paradoxical is implied in Professor Moltmann's thoughts also. The more we love life can we entertain death with dignity, the death of others and our own. "This other attitude toward death demands a process of education that removes the barriers of repression over against death and grief so that life again becomes worthy of love."[29]

In the process of reshaping the paradigms the imagination plays a most decisive role. It is the vehicle for the objectifying of the image which can then be turned into words, terms, concepts. An example of how imagination functions is derived from Professor Van Harvey's description of a "paradigmatic event."

> A paradigmatic event is one that fuses concreteness and a wider meaning. The more fundamental the meaning, the more the event becomes capable of being transformed into myth, where "myth" does not mean a false story but a highly selective story that is used to structure and convey the basic self-understanding of a community. A pattern is abstracted from the event and becomes the formalized parable that is used to interpret larger tracts of history and experience. This parable is preserved and retold in order to reaffirm the faith and values of the community

and to communicate them to its young. The images derived from it constitute the key to that community's elemental confidences.[30]

Imagination is the method in man of using these events to the construction of general truths, systems, ideologies, etc. Imagination lifts dominant points of reference out of a content to a level of importance. These are paradigmatic events composed of many elements of existence.[31] Applying this method to the reconstruction of religion is to see, for example, biblical events, as paradigmatic events held in esteem by Judaic and Christian believers as worthy of helping man live in the image of God's love. Further, imagination allows man to choose selectively, beyond the limitation of traditional biblical interpretations, images of God most conducive to a life of qualitative authenticity, for the events of the Bible enable man to "image the real." According to Martin Buber "imaging the real" takes place only in the lived concrete, in the address and response of I-Thou.[32]

It is my conviction that meeting the events recorded in the Scriptures provides a possibility for man authentically to transcend the temporality and particularity of the event. Transcendence may be realized through a method for reshaping paradigms in the light of man's present ontological, experiential, and epistemological ethical paradox. In this meeting he can then take the events seriously, as having meaning, and also imagine the evolving revelation of man with God in images adapted to the kind of life our sciences, technology, and psychosocial behavior have taught us about ourselves. That in no way dismisses the function of "myth," or "story," or the question of the idea of God. Professor Buri discusses the place of myth in a statement which can be applied to the ethical paradox of the relation between "God" and man.

> Without mythological discourse about the voice which calls us to responsibility, we cannot achieve clarity concerning the essence of the unconditionedness of responsibility. It goes without saying that the voice addresses us in our language, arises in our hearts, speaks to us from out of our surroundings; and yet, it is not merely the voice of my heart, my neighbor, my situation. In the objectivity of our inner and outer world, there is no

unconditionedness, but only demonstrable relativity. To be sure, we must not overlook the relativity of our objective world be-because it serves for the proper enactment of the unconditioned-ness of our personhood. But in the midst of these relativities occurs the voice, without the awareness of which we do not achieve personhood.[33]

However, mythological discourse is not merely the voice which addresses us; it is also that power in man—imagination—con-cretizing this persuasive force. Professor Gilkey describes the epistemology of the myth-making function in man. "Myth concerns . . . man's power through critical inquiry, scientific con-clusions, and a sensible moral use of his knowledge to create a new environment outside him and a new nature for himself, and thus to control by his own intelligence and moral will the forces outside and inside man that heretofore have determined him."[34] Theodore Roszak emphasizes the negative value of myths. They are the "imaginative exaggerations of our ordinary perceptions or displacement of them to other times and places" which reflect the objectification of consciousness producing: "1) the alienative dichotomy; 2) the invidious hierarchy; 3) the mechanistic im-perative."[35] Their positive function, on the other hand, is their universality and the fact that men need myths to ground and support their values and ideals.[36]

Myths carry moral implications, and usually justify our present conduct. According to Edmund Leach, anthropologist, myths are ambiguous. "People who use a religious story for a mythical pur-pose always talk as if the implications of the story are obvious. But different preachers use the same story to produce different moral injunctions. . . ."[37] Yet, when put together in a religious system, the contradictions embedded in myths fit together to form para-digms and create the ambiguity wherein metaphysical truth resides. The message, then, may defy (and I might add, defraud) the story line.[38] However, this purpose can be lost in the major side effect of mythology—whether it be the myth of the American Dream, the myth of the happy marriage or the mythical tales of religious charisma. "For since it has always been on myths that the moral orders of societies have been founded, the myths canonized as religion, and since the impact of science on myths results—apparently inevitably—in moral disequilibrium, we must now ask whether it is not possible to arrive *scientifically* at such an understanding of life-supporting nature of myths that, in criticizing their archaic features, we do not misrepresent and disqualify their necessity. . . ."[39] For myths contain archetypes, i.e., "primordial implantations," "implanted, stamped, engraved from the beginning."[40]

Where are the archetypes? Some may say in the depths, some nowhere, others in themselves, still others, like Carl Jung, in the *collective* unconscious or, "that they are known or rather that we know them only in symbolic conjunctions."[41] The archetype further functions to unify the activity of the imagination in constructs which are communicable and operable whether in analytic psychology, such as Professor Jung practiced, or religious images. According to Professor Hart, the archetype represents a "nondiscursive similitude of *form* in historical manhood."[42] Form is the limiting pattern which the archtype defines. "Man's being-in-the-world is characterized by two sorts of limitations or relative fixity: the fixity of his appetite and the fixity of cosmic pattern. Archetypal images may therefore be said to be the nondiscursive embodiment of the interaction between man's fixity of appetite and the fixity of pattern in the cosmos.[43] Establishing the bipolar limits for the ontological structure of man in the world with his desire or need within the order/chaos in the cosmos, Professor Hart like Professor Whitehead suggests a mediation point for the function of the principle of fixity. Professor Hart calls it imagination; Professor Whitehead, I believe, calls it decision-making (to be discussed in a later section). Perhaps myth must be seen as a real constituent of the function of man's imagination, to be used to construct a dialectical world view prompted by the urgings of the inner man and "the voice beyond." Although it is constructed by men, myth is still necessary for the memorable paradigms and archetypes it recalls by (1) stressing their importance in the form of human history, (2) pointing beyond themselves (transcendence), and (3) calling for reshaping in the passage of time, progress, and culture.

Importance as a key construct, adapted from the philosophy of Professor Alfred North Whitehead, places emphasis on those paradigms which retain their meaning by relating to the needs and concrete issues of a specific time and place. Because of its significance as an epistemological parameter, I will discuss Whitehead's emphasis in a separate chapter. The basis for the selection of this concept is found in the principle of process itself. The principle of process which he offers is stated in his "categories of explanation" in *Process and Reality*. "That *how* an actual entity becomes constitutes *what* that actual entity *is*; so that the two descriptions of an actual entity are not independent. Its 'being' is constituted by its 'becoming.' This is the 'principle' of 'process.' "[44] This process-principle motivates both his ontology and his epistemology. The process-principle is grounded in a deep conviction.

> Progress in truth—truth of science and truth of religion—is mainly a progress in the framing of concepts, in discarding artificial abstractions or partial metaphors, and in evolving notions which strike more deeply into the root of reality.[45]

To transcend means to preserve the integrity of the past while at the same time to attend meaningfully to the present. The consequences of this transcendence are to discard doctrines, laws, morals, images of God and man influenced by other times and other cultures simply as traditionally "acceptable." Transcendence allows room for the imagination to seek the positive function of assuming a more formal activity of creating by reshaping discarded ideas into that which is called the "immortal" in man— his striving for belief. A man who sees himself not as the master of nature but as the director of nature in a salvific wholeness; a man who sees his weakness not as a willful sin but as natural limitations is able to be his own focus and thus to be able to respond. Transcendence also points to the possibility of a God subject to limitation simply because he is known as he is known. To hypothesize a metaphysically perfect Being is not a viable option given the human functions of imagination and cognition. Transcendence allows a correlation *between man's knowledge* (and lack of knowledge) and his *power of describing the visible and invisible realities he experiences or intuits.*

The entire project of educational rehabilitation involves man in a perspective change, a change grounded in a response of value priorities rooted in reshaped paradigms and firmed-up parameters (value ontology). We must convince man that he is in a ground of operability which demands a *wisdom of method* as much, if not more, than our religious forebears realized. Value ontology is not a convenient approach to the meeting of religion and ethics. It is the product of a genuine attempt to understand where man is today. In the area of ethics *man lies beyond a defined responsibility to or for something or someone.* For some this means he is nowhere. On the contrary, *to be beyond responsibility is to be nearer to a wisdom of a response of value.*

> We are today the multiplied images of a single
> man in all his
> wonderful contradictions,
> astride an unsettled land, driven,
> wild and willful, toward
> the dreamed immortal meaning of a home.
> We balance in a savage equipoise
> between our myths and
> actualities: a land of lofty principle and crystal pristine pureness
> where no ecstasies are alien; the soul Victorian in the body
> world. But always that within us most childlike, grave, eager and
> unappeasable drives us on.[46]

Through memory, forgetfulness, and imagination I have described the elements which point to an ontology of valuing. Through importance and transcendence the valuing itself takes place as man is cognizant of his multiple images in a culture of innovation. However, the method which I have so far described must be tested in the area of ethics.

From situation ethics to de-ontological ethics to a phenomenological approach to ethics, man has been bombarded by a rationalization of man's active, constructive place in nature with and without reference to spiritual factors. Responsibility has replaced the command to do good and avoid evil. "Responsibility" appears, at first hand, to have a broad range of possibilities, yet in actuality responsibility has a determinate focus. Man is responsible to . . . ; man is responsible for. . . . Although man has lost the rigid determination of absolute values, he has replaced them with the flexibility of the situation and/or context dictating a sense of responsibility to be answered by reshaped paradigms arising from operable constructs. Man has now gone beyond responsibility to a keener scrutiny of what he is about and what is about him.

> "Responsibility" presupposes the fully developed ability to "respond" as a person. But there are many stages of reduced centeredness caused by tiredness, sickness, intoxication, neurotic compulsions, and psychotic splits. All this does not remove responsibility, but it shows the element of destiny in every act of freedom. . . . One of the most striking facts about the dynamics of the human personality is the intentional ignorance concerning one's real motives. The motives themselves are bodily and psychic strivings, often far removed from what appears as conscious reason in a centered decision. Such a decision is still free, but it is freedom within the limits of destiny. . . . The centered self is dependent not only on the influences of its social surroundings which are consciously given and received but also on those which are effective in a society without being apprehended and formulated. All this shows that the independence within an individual decision is only half the truth.[47]

Man is appreciating himself in his paradoxical socio-psychological environment, searching for wisdom—authentic living in all aspects of his being, especially in religion, creating new symbols of process by risking experimentation in such areas as biomedical ethics and the psychology of self, and the inquiry into power and control. Traditionally accepted roles such as president, politician, minister, priest, nun, psychiatrist and psychotherapist, social worker and teacher are being recast and remolded. All of these factors have resulted in responses of value to unique, concrete situations. The gap between the innocent and the guilty man, and, the ideal and the real, which religion has so often expressed in its paradigms, must be closed. For we do not know where responsibility begins and ends in human evolution.[48]

Specific values have conspicuously emerged with priorities, such as integrity, respect for scientific progress and human limitation, and tolerance, as the reshaping of paradigms have unconsciously been taking place. But they have only evolved from specific conflicts. Religions must evoke the same priorities toward life. First, religion must seriously extend its borders to the ethical, thus discarding morality, with a *reconstructed* sense of what man is doing when he is being religious; second, it must assert the importance of the process of life discoveries; third, it must separate the individual from the social to discover guidelines for issues and thus highlight decision-making. What religion must find is a common universe of discourse through a sound methodological approach to issues of serious concern among the basic values man-in-culture seeks.

I concur with Professor Fontinell that

> there would seem therefore to be a need for an ethic which is accessible and helpful to a certain range of contemporary man. This ethic must allow for diversity, even diversity of fundamental beliefs, but must not lead to a destructive division of men into isolated, ghettoized, or antagonistic groups. This ethic must not be simply the lowest common denominator of those values on which most men agree. Rather, it must include the diversities in such a way that men from different cultures and traditions can interact so that the human situation will be continually enriched. Such an ethics would even be capable of involving a plurality of religious perspectives.[49]

These religious perspectives, however, must function in "fields" of operability, i.e., "constellation of focused relations,"[50] in which responses of value enable an ontology (i.e., the *structure* of focused relations) to appear.

> . . . The human person does not exist as an isolated atom but is actually *constituted* by his relationships—to the world, to his family, to his fellow men, to the Church and to God. It is important to stress that these relationships are not extrinsic or spatial but intrinsic: they belong to the very fabric of the person's being. Further, these relationships are not given once and for all. . . . The free acts whereby he creates his relationships— in such instances as marriage or having children—make him a "new" man. The ethical principle suggested by all of this is that any human decision-making process must strive to be as faithful as possible to the totality of the person and must avoid

centering on one aspect of the person in isolation from other equally important aspects.[51]

Such is the operational model of a healthy religious outlook. Within religious diversity, the operational principle of "something is what it does" is derived from (1) the model or format of the activity, (2) the environment in which the activity occurs, (3) the persons in relation to (1) and (2), and (4) the effects of the process itself. The process, then, of relating to the operational principle gives rise to the active engagement of the persons in the only solitary activity, i.e., decision-making.

Professor Whitehead's description of decision-making in a Gestalt of relations amplifies the meaning of fields by focusing the element which transcends the model and conditions creativity by "cutting off" other possibilities. This description follows from an amplification of the notion of "givenness."

> For rationalistic thought, the notion of "givenness" carries with it a reference beyond the mere data in question. It refers to a "decision" whereby what is "given" is separated off from what for that occasion is "not given." This element of "givenness" in things implies some activity procuring limitation. The word "decision" does not here imply conscious judgment, though in some "decisions" consciousness will be a factor. The word is used in its root sense of a "cutting off." The ontological principle declares that every decision is referable to one or more actual entities, because in separation from actual entities there is nothing, merely nonentity—"The rest is silence."
>
> The ontological principle asserts the relativity of decision; whereby every decision expresses the relation of the actual thing, *for which* a decision is made, to an actual thing *by which* that decision is made. But "decision" cannot be construed as a casual adjunct of an actual entity. It constitutes the very meaning of actuality. An actual entity arises from decisions *for* it, and by its very existence provides decisions *for* other actual entities which supersede it. Thus the ontological principle is the first stage in constituting a theory embracing the notions of "actual entity," "givenness," and "process." Just as "potentiality for process" is the meaning of the more general term "entity," or "thing," so "decision" is the additional meaning imported by the word "actual" into the phrase "actual entity." "Actuality" is the decision amid "potentiality." It represents stubborn fact

which cannot be evaded. The real internal constitution of an actual entity progressively constitutes a decision conditioning the creativity which transcends that actuality.[52]

At that one moment the decision is the limiting factor as well as the positive force. In the process of evaluation the decisive step produces the only permanence in the transitional phases of this world. Paradoxically, as the Buddhist would have it, desire is that which limits and causes suffering, yet the wanting for nothing is itself desire; thus stillness is the only unwilled movement of time and self. Within and without the time and space of our world, we cannot idealize the world by seeking the refuge of simplicity, mere virtue, or the return of the good old days. In the process of reshaping our paradigms, reordering our constructs, firming up our parameters and maintaining our fields of operability, we can use a refined sense of technocracy for the purpose of the maintenance of value priorities but only if these are revealed in the *fields* created yet not completed by existential concreteness. From Martin Buber's I-Thou relation, to Paul Tillich's courage in the face of the shock of nonbeing and in spite of man's limitations, to Pierre Teilhard de Chardin's hominization process of the community of mankind, man must express a further dimension of operability—not adequately met by pure existentialist idealism.[53]

The seventies, on the other hand, are a time for a realism that refuses to deny the hard facts of behaviorism, technocracy, eugenic and genetic engineering—all of which demand a modified behaviorism, a mixture of the valuable, the personal, and efficiency, i.e., operability. Existentialist ideals are without method. On the individual level, the existential position may be adequate. In a social context, it bears little fruit except the spontaneity of the moment and that is shortlived in this culture. Perhaps when Paul Tillich observed, *"What was essentially intended in the theological system of ethics can only be realized by means of a theology of culture applying not only to ethics but to all the functions of culture; not a theological system of ethics, but a theology of culture,"*[54] his words may be extended to include, not simply theology, but ethics, religion, and culture as the field of operability for the function of ethics. But what of religion in this cultural explosion?

One premise under which we must work is that religion cannot be divorced from life as it is lived. *To know where religion is one must know where we are in life and where life is in us.* To create the construct of life, man, God, creation, etc. in a truly representative and meaningful way, man must expose the very strengths he guards so carefully. Existentialism is a case in point.

> When the ultimate basis of our world is in question, we run to different holes in the ground, we scurry into roles, statuses, identities, interpersonal relations. We attempt to live in castles that can only be in the air because there is no firm ground in the social cosmos on which to build.[55]

Fear is no longer the existential fear of the individual in the face of neurotic anxiety, but it is the cosmic anguish from which every reflective man suffers when he tries to fathom the complexities of the paradox which he lives. In comprehending that paradox he must reconstruct his "firm ground." For those for whom the divine was that ground, the divine is now a model constructed from the paradigms of a continuously moving world of action, stopped only by a momentary decision from time to time. The divine then comes to mean to be lost beyond the time-space continuity of a single event or thought. Transcending the particular events with which we want to identify the construct "divinity," the construct itself is rooted in the complex of world religious experience, that is, a complex of human, psychosocial, cultural, historical, and "wholly other" experience. Thus, divinity is "Relating Itself" and not merely a substantive concept implied by those who employ the term. As one source of the ethical paradox, the question of divinity could be viewed in our contemporary world as reshaped, after the paradigm of the Judeo-Christian story, into covenant by function, the model consisting of the series of covenantal relationships in the Hebrew Scriptures and in the New Testament, informing the knowledge and image of man, as well as man's desire to continue the transcendent appreciation of "otherness." Theologies, religious experiences, figures of religious significance, such as Jesus, Buddha, Socrates, Gandhi, Self, represent mediational truths in the process of "truthing" which is the consequence of decision-making. Divinity then becomes, with the aid of mediational truths, a qualitative way of functioning in the field of operability. Discerning limits and possibilities through the environment (knowledge and physical) becomes the search for meaning.

Very few religious writers in the West have seen an organic relationship between the religious and the ethical. Professor Max Kadushin, a rabbinic scholar, relates the organic and the ethical in a construct *Derek Erez.*

> By means of the concept *Derek Erez* all acts characteristic of humanity were *potentially* included within the response of the ethical; when such acts were grasped or interpreted by a fundamental concept they were *actually* within the scope of the ethical. Again, certain persistent human traits such as love, humility, arrogance, truthfulness and so on were regarded as always *actually* within the scope of the ethical; and being aspects of *Derek Erez*, served as sub-concepts of the latter in the organic complex and were likewise integrated within the fundamental concepts. The sphere of the ethical was, therefore, in a sense co-extensive with the sphere of characteristic, universal human conduct, a sphere so large as to have made the ethical meaningless had not *Derek Erez* been a concept within an organic complex. The organic complex in a continuous, living manner grasped now this and then that characteristic human act to draw it within the sphere of *Derek Erez*. The ethical, then, was not merely intertwined with the organic complex; without the organic complex there could have been no category of the ethical at all. This would seem to render futile the attempt to build up ethical systems in formulated, philosophical fashion, ethical systems that are not part of an integrated organic complex.
>
> Because the ethical concepts were part of the organic complex, the experience of God accompanied every concretization of an ethical concept.[56]

An organic view of life developed as a response to the inadequate mechanistic view of life. Mechanism has failed to show how the whole is more than the sum of the parts; the whole determines the nature of the parts (more than functionalism): the parts can only be understood if considered in relation to the whole; the parts are dynamically interdependent and interrelated. It is interesting to note that the roots of such an organistic philosophy is rooted not only in the Hebrew Bible but also in the Hindu scriptures—Vedas, Upanishads, and Bhagavad-Gita. Reality is seen as one with various emphases and levels of importance. (Gestalt psychology and psychotherapy have similar constructs as those found in organic thought as well as those found in operationalism.)

In reconstructing religious ethics I believe that we must take account of the nature of the organic complex with which we are concerned. The culture forms the mesh in which we catch facts and data through which values are labeled. But the inner dynamic of that which gives rise to values is a conceptual process both psychologically and religiously related. This dynamic renders such values as life, God, immortality as constructs which provide a transcendent meaning to the important paradigms of man's individual and social experience. These values guide our decision-making. Whatever we conceive them to be, values inform and construct our decision in its content. The phenomenology of making important is the next step toward a methodology for an operational process ethic.

NOTES

1. Maurice Friedman, influenced by the thought of Martin Buber, has provided a unique existential description of the "lived concrete" in the construct "Touchstones"; cf. *Touchstones of Reality: Existential Trust and the Community of Peace* (New York: E. P. Dutton, 1972).

2. Peter Homans in "The Future of Theology in a Mass Society," *Criterion* X, no. 3 (Spring 1971), p. 25, questions theology's capacity to reflect upon its own "social location," and "its capacity to adapt, reflectively, to social elements which attempt to force it to shift its social location one way or another." I would not use the term "theology" since it has a precise focus depending upon the denomination considered. Yet, I would say that *religion* must shift its "social location" so that theology might be done.

3. By the "valuable," I do not mean any essences existing a priori in nature. Rather I refer to what is found operating *between* man and the subject of his concern.

4. I am using the word "organic" as a philosophical attitude "proclaiming the need for reorganizing vast ranges of varieties of existing interdependencies and new complexities of principles already inherent in them" (Archie J. Bahm, "Organicism—A New World Hypothesis" [Albuquerque: University of New Mexico; reprinted from Memorias del XIII Congreso Internacional de Filosofía, Mexico City, IX, September 7–14, 1963], pp. 22–23). "Organicism's novelty consists, in part, in the *systematicness* with which it precommits itself, in part to the new theories which it generates,

in part in its predictive power regarding the kinds of theories which can be found relevantly acceptable about issues as well as in part, the novelty of its derivable (and predictable) *insights* relevant to each issue." Its key concepts are: (1) the relation and interdependence of experience and values, (2) the polarity of human experience—the limitations and possibilities of human experience, (3) dialectic or explanation, (4) the integrative power (organicity) of thought and action.

5. Cf. Kenneth Vaux, *Biomedical Ethics: Morality and the New Medicine* (New York: Harper & Row, 1974), pt. II, chap. 4, "Sources of Ethical Insight."

6. Ralph Wendell Burhoe, "Prophesying Human Value," in *Science and Human Value in the 21st Century*, ed. R. W. Burhoe (Philadelpha: Westminster Press, 1971), p. 27.

7. Ibid., p. 22.

8. Johannes B. Metz, "The Future *Ex Memoria Passionis*," in *Hope and the Future of Man*, ed. Ewert Cousins (Philadelphia: Fortress Press, 1972), p. 123.

10. See note 4, Chapter I.

11. Ian Barbour, *Science and Secularity: The Ethics of Technology* (New York: Harper & Row, 1970).

12. Ibid., pp. 26–27.

13. Ibid., p. 30.

14. Ian G. Barbour, *Myths, Models and Paradigms: A Comparative Study in Science and Religion* (New York: Harper & Row, 1974), p. 9.

15. Ibid., p. 6.

16. Ray L. Hart, *Unfinished Man and the Imagination: Toward an Ontology and Rhetoric of Revelation* (New York: Herder & Herder, 1968), p. 286.

17. Cf. Ibid., pp. 286–290.

18. Ibid., p. 287; cf. Barbour, *Myths, Models and Paradigms*, p. 148. Professor Barbour focuses on the exemplars who took part in historical occurrences more than on the events themselves.

19. Ibid., p. 287.

20. Cf. Barbour, *Science and Secularity*, pp. 10–32; *Myths, Models and Paradigms*, pp. 29–84.

21. Bernard J. F. Lonergan, "Theology and Man's Future," *Cross Currents* XIX, no. 4 (Fall 1969), p. 453.

22. Ibid., pp. 457–458.

23. Michael Novak, *Ascent of the Mountain, Flight of the Dove; An Invitation to Religious Studies* (New York: Harper & Row, 1971). In note 24, p. 215, Professor Novak asks us to compare Thomas S. Kuhn, *The Structure of Scientific Revolutions*, 2d ed. enlarged (Chicago: University of Chicago Press, 1972), Peter L. Berger and Thomas Luckmann, *The Social Construction of Reality: A Treatise on the Sociology of Knowledge* (Garden City: Doubleday, 1966); and Alfred Schutz, *The Phenomenology of the Social World*, trans. George Walsh and Frederick Lehmert (Evanston: Northwestern University Press, 1967).

24. Ibid., pp. 15–16.

25. Ibid.

26. Cf. Kenneth E. Boulding, *Beyond Economics* (Ann Arbor, Mich.: University of Michigan Press, 1970).

27. Cf. Augustine, *De Trinitate* (*The Trinity*), series: *The Fathers of the Church*, trans. Stephen McKenna, C. SS. R. (Washington, D.C.: Catholic University of America Press, 1963).

28. Jürgen Moltmann, "Hope and the Biomedical Future of Man," *Hope and the Future of Man*, ed. Ewert H. Cousins (Philadelphia: Fortress Press, 1972), p. 104.

29. Ibid.

30. Van A. Harvey, *The Historian and the Believer: The Morality of Historical Knowledge and the Christian Belief* (New York: Collier-Macmillan, 1969 [1966]).

31. See ibid., "Faith, Images and the Chrstian Perspective," for an illustration of this point in his discussion of the images of Jesus (pp. 275–276), and the complex question of what is a "religious" perspective.

32. Martin Buber, "Elements of the Interhuman," in *The Knowledge of Man*, ed. and introduction by Maurice Friedman (New York: Harper & Row, 1965), p. 81.

33. Fritz Buri, *How Can We Still Speak Responsibly of God?* trans. C. Hardwick (Philadelphia: Fortress Press, 1968), p. 27.

34. Langdon Gilkey, "Biblical Symbols in a Scientific Culture," in *Science and Human Values in the 21st Century,* ed. Ralph Wendell Burhoe (Philadlephia: Westminster Press, 1971), p. 80.

35. Theodore Roszak, *The Making of a Counter-Culture* (New York: Doubleday [Anchor], 1968), pp. 211, 217.

36. Cf. Joseph Campbell, *Myths to Live By*, foreword by Johnson E. Fairchild (New York: Viking Press, 1972), pp. 11–12.

37. Elizabeth Hall, "People Plan Their Lives in Terms of Imaginary Systems: Nobody Lives in the Real World—A Conversation with Edmund Leach," *Psychology Today* (July 1974), p. 68.

38. Ibid.

39. Campbell, *Myths to Live By*, pp. 11–12.

40. Hart, *Unfinished Man*, p. 290 and Carl Jung, *The Portable Jung*, ed. Joseph Campbell, trans. R. F. C. Hull (New York: Viking Press, 1971).

41. Hart, *Unfinished Man*, p. 290.

42. Ibid., p. 292.

43. Ibid., pp. 292–93.

44. *Process and Reality: An Essay in Cosmology* (New York: Harper Torchbooks, 1960; originally published by Macmillan, 1929), pp. 34–35. John Gaheen in Whitehead's "Theory of Value," in *The Philosophy of Alfred North Whitehead*, ed. Paul A. Schlipp, vol. III, The Library of Living Philosophers (Chicago: Northwestern University, 1941) states that Whitehead's ontology is based on his theory of value (p. 440).

45. Alfred North Whitehead, *Religion in the Making* (Cleveland: World Publishing Co., 1966 [Meridian Books, 1960]), p. 127.

46. William Hedgepett, "American Images," *Look* XXXIV, no. 14 (July 15, 1969).

47. Paul Tillich, *Systematic Theology*, vol. II (Chicago: University of Chicago Press, 1957), p. 42.

48. Ibid.

49. Eugene Fontinell, "Toward an Ethic of Relationships," in *Situationism and the New Morality*, ed. R. L. Cunningham (New York: Appleton-Century-Crofts, 1970), p. 204; cf. James F. Smurl, *Religious Ethics: A Systems Approach* (Englewood Cliffs, N.J.: Prentice-Hall, 1972). This is a text on comparative religious ethics. While it is a unique and comprehensive survey of world religious ethical perspectives, it provides no foundation for a method of decision-making common to each religion. The offer of a "people, process, principles" guide is an intra-religious perspective for understanding rather than a method for decision-making and ethical problem-solving.

50. Fontinell, "Toward an Ethic of Relationships," p. 207.

51. Eugene Fontinell, "Contraception and the Ethics of Relationships," in *What Modern Catholics Believe about Birth Control*, ed. William Birmingham (New York: Signet Books, 1964), p. 246; cf. n. 11. Professor Fontinell has based his position on both Kurt Lewin's "field theory" as well as Gardiner Murphy's definition of man in *Personality: A Biosocial Approach to Origins and Structure* (New York: Harper & Brothers, 1947), p. 7: "Man is a nodal region, an organized field within a larger field, a region of perpetual interaction, a reciprocity of outgoing and incoming energies."

52. Whitehead, *Process and Reality*, p. 68.

53. Cf. Barbara Ann DeMartino Swyhart, "*Value Ontology*: An Evaluation of Mordecai M. Kaplan's Philosophy of 'Wisdom,' " Ph.D. dissertation, Temple University, 1972.

54. Paul Tillich, "On the Idea of a Theology of Culture," in *What Is Religion?* ed. and with an introduction by James Luther Adams (New York: Harper Torchbooks, 1969), p. 160. Originally published in *Gesammelte Werke* (Stuttgart: Evangelisches Verlagswerk, n.d.).

55. Ronald D. Laing, *The Politics of Experience* (New York: Ballantine Books, 1967), p. 131.

56. Max Kadushin, *Organic Thinking: A Study in Rabbinic Thought* (New York: Jewish Theological Seminary of America, 1938), pp. 240–241.

III

Alfred North Whitehead
on "Importance" and "Value"

Religion is the vision of something which stands beyond, behind and within the passing flux of immediate things; something which is real, and yet waiting to be realized; something
which is a remote possibility, and yet the greatest of present
facts; something that gives meaning to all that passes and yet
eludes apprehension; something whose possession is the final
good, and yet is beyond all reach; something which is the ultimate ideal and the hopeless quest.[1]

Bioethical Decision-Making has been building a methodology for
an operational, process ethic. Thus far I have said little about the
process aspect of ethics. In this chapter I will suggest that Alfred
North Whitehead's philosophy of "importance" and "value" lends
a process perspective essential to the concretization of religious
ethics. The value ontology around which I structure decision-
making calls for a phenomenology of vision, or seeing what is
important in the shaping of values as operative for our time.
Alfred North Whitehead has most significantly contributed to this
vision. What follows is an extrapolation of his thought toward a
process ethic. Within the philosophy of Alfred North Whitehead
I find that an operational approach to the use of his creative constructs actually *does* what he theoretically suggests. It is possible
to couple a process ethic via value ontology with operationalism
in an effort to ground a methodology for bioethics. The specific
illustration of process ethics at work with which I will be concerned is the problematic of abortion; as I see it, the paradox of

ethical flexibility. The next chapter, "Reshaping the Religious toward Bioethics and Abortion," will discuss this meaningful problematic. This chapter focuses on man's process of valuing, the content of which is described by Whitehead as "religion."

As I have been using the construct "ethics," it may minimally be defined as the adequate meeting of conceptual justification(s) for actions and the actions themselves which are consequent to the justification(s). Too often ethics as a philosophic form sends ethicians in search of abstract theories. These theories seem to evade or lose sight of the *concrete* ground of "where men actually are." It is "where men actually are" that Professor Whitehead begins.

Religion provides man with an expression of "character," a complex of value experiences which give a sense of unity to man's life. Value experiences result from the coordination of one's awareness of possible variations of behavior and belief. Coordination of value experiences, then, is the result of the process of decision-making. Ideally, the process results in a single response pattern of one's individual "character."

Ethics, religion, and psychology are distinct responses to the human pattern of life, memory, forgetfulness, and transcendence, including those aspects of the epistemological parameters which demand a specific rhythm, such as belief, death, and immortality. Within a "common universe of discourse" each discipline responds to the concrete facts of individual experience by a re-creation of values in various patterns or by a readjustment of values—centering that effort within the human power of organization. The results of this power of organization are individual and societal convictions, conceptualized as important.

Alfred North Whitehead's contribution to the individual and cultural problematic of man's wholeness lies (1) in the realization of his value epistemology and (2) in an understanding of the process of "making important" within a process philosophy. I will refer to this methodology by the construct "value ontology." I want to establish: (1) the process methodology by which Whitehead has spoken to the cultural occasions of ethical needs and psychological insight; (2) the attitudes which process ethics and process psychology foster in the *practical,* individual and cultural concerns of ethics and psychology. It is this process methodology which becomes the ground for decision-making in the midst of ethical paradox.

The creation of "active novelty" for the purpose of "illuminating the social system" gives a definite function to the endless task of the rational ordering of life. This purpose which I have called a "functional value ontology," or a "dynamic" within specified fields of operability, such as the biomedical field, is derived from the organic nature of entities themselves.[2] A functional value ontology seeks to express that "aim" which Whitehead terms "civilization," which is a "fineness of feeling" through the arrangement of "its social relations, and the relations of its members to their natural environment, as to evoke into the experiences of its members Appearances dominated by the harmonies of forceful enduring things."[3] Civilization, however, is only functionally operable if each individual is in tune with the "deep recesses of feeling" which occur within the various patterns of civilization itself (i.e., patterns of behavior, patterns of emotion, patterns of belief, and technologies). Civilization is a conception of social and cultural unity. This expression—"fineness of feeling"—is part of the ontological sphere since it represents the "ontological principle"—"that every condition to which the process of becoming conforms in any particular instance has its reason either in the character of some actual entity in the actual world of that concrescence [that is, "the fluency inherent in the constitution of the particular existent"] *or* in the character of the subject which is in the process of concrescence."[4] Whitehead states:

> This ontological principle means that actual entities (self-interested, self-valuated entities) are the only *reasons* so that to search for a *reason* is to search for one or more actual entities. It follows that any condition to be satisfied by one actual entity in its process expresses a fact either about "the real internal constitutions" of some other actual entities or about the "subjective aim" conditioning the process.[5]

Translating this technical language into the recognizable signs of our problematic, I might say that the roots of current dilemmas are to be found within the analysis of the character or purpose of actual entities whether they be persons or situations. Discovering the unity of character within the diversity of actual occasions which make up a concrescence seems to be the general purpose of the philosophic endeavor.[6] The application of this general observation to the practical areas of contemporary problems suggests the principle of process as the unfolding paradox of data and values. Therefore, in order to see into a situation one must participate in that situation as becoming with it whatever it has come to be at the moment that it is grasped as a problem, as a disvalue, or a disharmony, i.e., that which is inadequate to the task at hand. To grasp the problematic of biomedical ethics and decision-making one must take account of the data and values involved before superimposing other data and new values. The field of operation for this accountability is self-consciousness.

The value experience develops as one participates in the "awareness process" signified by Whitehead as the activity of prehension. The activity of prehension of actual occasions results in an "epochal occasion," an "arrest" realized in the actualization of one event within the duration of a field consisting of a realized pattern noticeably the character of an event.[7] The process of valuing involves: (1) the *power*[8] of the individual's experience, (2) the degree or level of *"importance,"*[9] made possible by the (3) *perspective* given to the facts of the occasion, (4) contributing to the process of *abstraction* (that is, going beyond the data), that is, realizing ideal forms within occasions or, in other words, concrete instances of the exemplification of what we commonly call ideals or ideal values.[10] The process is mediated by the "I" of the value experience. "I" value facts as elements of the whole organic complex. The power of the importance of the facts as a totality consequently demands a transcendent value which I am free to give or not to give to the experience. In this choice I either immortalize or destroy a value, but the process continues.

What then determines the level of importance? Not only the process which I have outlined, but also two fundamental aspects of the personality of the "I": (1) emotion, i.e., response value; (2) self-consciousness. The result of the process is to return to the concrete totality for the reshaping of a paradigm, articulated as a construct, a value experience important to the "I"[11] The process begins and ends in the concrete. There is no ultimate end— simply the intrinsic worth of the process itself.

Abstraction through the prehension of concrete data is accomplished as a function of reason. "Reason is the organ of emphasis upon novelty. It provides the judgment by which it (novelty) passes into realization in purpose, and thence its realization in fact.[12] Reason suggests "the way of rhythm," the movement of the universe, a fundamental movement toward aesthetic satisfaction.[13] It is interesting to note that we may find out more about the nature of *reason* in Whitehead's ontology by pointing to its *antithesis—fatigue*. The suggestion, I believe, is that that which excludes the impulse toward the novel is not the rational.[14] Contrary to some who have ideas of Whitehead's affinity for Greek paradigms, the idea of Fatigue changes the meaning of Reason from the intellectual apprehension of truth to the *active exercise* of novel forms in the process of the ordering of things. Reason functions then as an ambitious, pragmatic epistemology to organize finite experiences. Its justification is sought in the *success* of the conceptualization and harmonization of our accounts of various kinds of experience.[15] The endurance of patterns throughout this process is a definite clue to the psychological dimensions of self, society, and civilization, to the ethical demand for continuity within change,[16] and to their common universe of discourse. It is in the area of the endurance of realized patterns of activity that the problematic of personal identity defines itself in my terms of (1) lack of "ego immediacy" and (2) lack of "adjustment prehensions."[17] Ego immediacy refers to the shock of the real life situation. A lack of adjustment prehensions is our basic resistance to adaptation to fundamental change. Precisely this second element is the inability of the "I" to coordinate its adjustment prehensions finitely, and erroneously leads to "value" construed as a final concept, the final goal, a *fait accompli,* rather than as the illustration of the finite unitive character of the processive world of fact.[18] The responsibility for "ego immediacy" and "adjustment prehension" rests with the "I" in its process of "making important."

Paradoxically, the unity among actual occasions is further occasioned by the "principle of concretion" or "limitation," a construct adequately represented by God's function in the world of fact and the world of value. To this principle of concretion, Whitehead attributes: (1) individualization into a multiplicity of modes and (2) the realm of the eternal objects which are variously synthesized in these modes. Given these conditions, limitation is implied in finiteness. Further, actual occasions contain modes of existence. Modes are limited by (1) special logical relations, (2) the selection of relationships, and (3) the particularity of the course of events.[19] Modes are created by choice and limited by their own multiplicity. Through choice or antecedent selection, future modal pluralities receive a specific determination. Modes themselves may have standards implicit in them from past occasions other than perhaps the intentions for which they were chosen. Modes may be concretely exemplified by moral directions, pace-setters, normative criteria which are limited by the qualifications just mentioned. Thus, they, too, are again limited. Whitehead states this another way: "Restriction is the price of value."[20] Limitation operates with prior standards, reversing their importance.

> There cannot be value without antecedent standards of value, to discriminate the acceptance or rejection of what is before the envisaging mode of activity. Thus there is an antecedent limitation among values, introducing contraries, grades, and oppositions.[21]

Moral standards, like all individual and societal realities demand the process of reconstruction in the light of this fact: Restriction is the price of value. Put another way, even the most absolute of principles is subject to the "tacit dimension" of the process itself.

The ultimate limitation of course is God—for whom no reason can be given, yet from whom all reason flows. "God is the ultimate limitation, and His existence is the ultimate irrationality. For no reason can be given for just that limitation which it stands in his nature to impose. God is not concrete, but He is the ground for concrete actuality. No reason can be given for the nature of God, because that nature is the ground of rationality."[22] With the same reasoning, Whitehead raises the question of "evil" as a two-edged sword—both as *"limitation"* and as the "aim to moral order." This does not, as some would believe, merely reinforce the adage that "good may come out of evil," but rather that limitation of itself suggests finiteness, restriction, and obviously a lack of harmony. Reasons for such elements are in the nature of occasions rather than in the a priori rationalism reminiscent of seventeenth-century thinkers. In the Whiteheadian order of things the limitless limit is the only possibility of man and God, separately and together. May I add that ethics, psychology, and religion deal most acutely with "limitless limits." Thus, limitation is precisely the *positive* prod toward the operability and applicability of process thought. Impermanence, reversals of thoughts and aims, processive insights through decision-making, and responsible grouping of occasions are the characteristics of the value seeker in the dimensions of ethics, psychology, and religion (as I have distinguished it from spirituality).[23] Even the construct "evil" demonstrates the limitation prodding us to secure the harmony of world moral order.

> The common character of all evil is that its realization in fact involves that there is some concurrent realization of purpose toward elimination. The purpose is to secure the avoidance of evil. The fact of the instability of the world is the moral order of the world.[24]

Nothing, therefore, can pull us away from the active participation in the existence that we possess. Man is limited finitely to the world of possibility, to the ordering of facts and values, to the coordination of his particular total environment as it changes with expanding concepts of the self and the culture. But, what precisely are values in the context of making important and in relation to the ethical paradox?

Value like the concept of "importance" can mean various

things.[25] It can mean, as I have shown, the limitation or standard which is antecedent to a particular occasion. Value can refer to the "locus of relational possibilities" which again implies the twofold dynamic of realized limit and creative potential expressed as "relevance of value."[26] In terms of the content of an event or an occasion, value can refer to the process of interest or enjoyment which accrues to the self.[27] Thus, value is the ground— a conceptual and emotional ground— from which the "I" derives grades and levels of what interest generates as "important" (value ontology). In this ground religion finds its function as that which is a "a moment of self-consciousness" represented by the movement from emptiness to adversity to relationship which involves the intuition of the ultimate character of the universe. Conceptually, these occasions reveal: (1) the value of the individual for itself, (2) the value of diverse individuals for each other, and (3) the value of the objective world. The "objective world" is a community derivative from the interrelations of its component individuals. It is necessary for the valued existence of each of these individuals.[28] But values themselves are specific. They are "created units of feeling arising out of the specific mode of concretion of the diverse elements. These different specific value feelings are comparable amid their differences and the ground for this compatibility is what is here termed 'value.' "[29] This coming together of universal-individual is what Whitehead calls the "revelation of character." Character, inherent in the nature of things, is discovered by the subjective involvement of the "I" through the decision process. The principle of this coming together or movement is an "intuition of immediate occasions" as failing or succeeding in reference to the ideal relevant to them. In this connection Professor Whitehead stated: "There is a rightness attained or missed, with more or less completeness of attainment or omission."[30] The acquisition of character is the revelation of relation, experiencing each moment of the quest in our solitariness, relating that to and from others and the objective world, deriving value from each event or moment, and continuing onward in the process of discovering the ideal amid becoming perfection.[31]

The interconnection of facts, feelings, grades of relevance or importance ("that aspect of feeling whereby a perspective is imposed upon the universe of things felt"), and perspective give rise to the selection of values related in the organismic process. As Whitehead says, "There is no entity, not even God, 'which requires nothing but itself in order to exist.' "[32] The world, then, is essentially social. Each entity requires the totality in order to exist and the totality requires each entity, unique in its mode, its value, and its own identity. "In fact, the society for each entity, actual or ideal, is the all-inclusive universe, including its ideal forms."[33] Persuasion through the mediation of coordinated, active creativity characterizes a universe of value.[34] It is this function which the concept of God further symbolizes.

God is "the valuation of the world."[35]

> God is that *function* in the world by reason of which our purposes are directed to ends which in our consciousness are impartial as to our own interests. He is that element in virtue of which judgment stretches beyond facts of existence to values of existence. He is that element in virtue of which our purposes extend beyond values for ourselves to values for others. He is that element in virtue of which the attainment of such a value for others transforms itself into value for ourselves.[36]

God and value are intimately related as the ground for thoughtful activity for "all value is the gift of finitude which is the necessary condition of actuality."[37] Creation itself is the self-limitation of God—his own restriction, chosen and tending toward his self-consciousness. Advance and novelty are at one and the same time causes and products of his immanence and transcendence. God depends on the universe. The binding together of the subjective aim of the world with the consequent nature of God who is completed by the "individual, fluent satisfaction of finite fact" is the wisdom Whitehead offers as a goal in his philosophy of organism.[38] Value, then, because of the constant ingress[39] of forms in the world of fact, *becomes* the ground of actuality, i.e., the potential within actualities as well as the correlate effects of actualities, expressed partly by moral judgments.[40]

The worth of Whitehead's organismic value theory, which I have described as "value ontology," lies in its *qualitative* approach to civilization. We are now in the broader *totality* of which the individual "I" is a microcosm. This qualitative character is important from four perspectives: (1) its emphasis upon feeling is the expression of needs and wants through the mediation of choice rather than force; (2) its ready acceptance of limitation as inherent in the character of the world of experience (pluralistic) and the world of value (multiplicity); (3) its inclusion of the realm of possibility issuing in novel forms surrounded by change and impermanence so necessary in the growth of ethical, religious, and psychological responses; (4) the emphasis upon relativity which is implied in 1, 2, and 3. As a social "field" civilization maintains patterns which coordinate the world of fact and the world of value. Consciousness as "value-feeling in depth" strengthens man against the "artificiality of an occasion of experience."[41] It is only by the strength of the value feeling that man can constantly and unceasingly attempt the harmony of contrasting elements of harmony and discord. Symbolic expressions—religious (creeds), ethical (commandments), psychological (imaginings), paradigmatic events and/or models and constructs—serve to exemplify the operability of the value-feeling.[42]

The process of "becoming" as a complex of interrelations of individuals in the world is a complex of radical flux and moments of consciousness. When the process is halted by statements, fixed orders, codes or static images of God or man, the result is inhibiting and inhibited activity, lack of progress and lack of growth. Whether we apply this to religion, to ethics, or to psychology, the outcome is the same. The process is halted only by decisions which seem to create irreversibility and permanence. Qualifying our actions and thoughts by the becoming process offers the growth in change that for too many produces the fear of instability— unnecessary because it is based on a misinformed idea of the nature of man, God, and reality. It would be natural for Whitehead, as he does, to find that the "fineness of feeling" which characterizes the civilizational goal resides in the aesthetic quality of life rather than in the moral fiber of life. For it is most difficult to relate concepts of self-consciousness and social consciousness to any existing concept of ethics, morality, or social psychology. And yet, his thought is precisely directed in the path of ethics—individual and social—and psychology—personal and social.

I have attempted to expose the conceptual framework and operability of an organic value ontology, defined by process and controlled by the value experience of the "I," who is at one and the same time individual and social. The consequences of such a position as Whitehead's persuades us to focus on the process of selectivity. The process of selectivity is successful, however, only on the basis of its attunement or harmony with the individual and social dilemmas of particular cultural occasions. Thus, Whitehead has led us both into responsible thought and action and beyond responsibility in any presently understood sense. The process of selectivity—the phenomenology of "making important" —directs us to responses of self-consciousness by choices which are conditioned by the temporal-historical and the transcendent-immanent poles of process. Activity is value activity, the act of becoming or choosing "something." "I" function truly when I am aware of the limitations and possibilities of the existence—past, present, and future—which "I" am. This is value ontology. A value ontology persuades us in the directions of a self-conscious adventure, an adventure shared by ethics, religion, and psychology.

I believe in the commission which Whitehead has given us: we must incorporate vague and disorderly elements of experience; otherwise the advance into novelty or existence is meaningless.[43] I must then accept his challenge to reconstruct the unity of concrescence in the evaluation process, first by seeking that unity in the individual "I," and second, by assessing the "value feeling(s)" of the broader social context. I offer some suggestions for a unity of concrescence in the individual incorporating "ego immediacy" and "adjustment prehensions" in a concept of the "I."

With regard to the psychology of the individual: (1) "I" am the mediator between reality and my functioning within reality. My particular needs and wants are in fact why the "I" chooses as it does. Prehensions, intensity of feelings, and value experiences direct my "rationale" for a life style. (2) Values are hermeneutically functional—if they are actualized at all. The operability of the value feeling for good or for ill is contingent upon the level of awareness of the "I" accompanying the actualization process. "I" must interpret values as positive or negative from the perspective of my self-consciousness. In the light of the function of values, education of the self-conscious process is more important than set patterns of techniques, therapies, norms, dogmas or creeds.

The above considerations relate to the ethical actualization of the self-conscious "I." Ethics and psychology, once again, are twins born of the same parents. (1) "I" am not a combination of fragmented experiences. Within the possible, diverse perspectives of the individual, his uniqueness is contingent upon the personal identity of a sequence of immediate moments. Only "I" can realize the sequence and imagine the continuum in the process itself. (2) Impermanence, flexibility, the polarities of limitation and possibility within a personal identity compromise the paradoxical ground of the process of selfhood. Attending decisions provide the reflective and integrative patterns which, at one and the same time, insure rest and motion. (3) Only through concrete, actual occasions can "I" define values (and disvalues) which are such only for a limited sequence within the process. Through the process of the formation of perspective *"I" discern the values which create me by persuading me to create them.* (4) Consciousness of desire, or value-feeling, and deliberate choice can free the "I" from the guilt of "past" failures and omissions. Without this deliberateness man cannot proceed holistically in the process as an actual occasion.

The ramifications of such conceptual possibilities of the limited "I" within the social context to produce a social ethic or social psychology are quite distinct from the individual consequences I have mentioned. Social ethics and social psychology cannot operate on the fluency described above because of the built-in control factors of sophisticated societies. Individuals must seek values often amid conflicting systems. Nevertheless, these factors must be raised to the necessary power within a civilizational milieu of appropriate value-feelings. I do not agree with Whitehead that aesthetic appreciation is a sufficient goal within the complex cultural occasions we face. Yet, the descriptive quality of Whitehead's categories is applicable to the world-at-large. I make this statement knowing well that the consequences are more difficult to discern in the areas of practical operability. I would like to offer a few suggestions for a socio-ethical psychology and suggest the limitations of such a theory.

(1) The psychology of a society is contingent upon diverse and pluralistic perspectives which give rise to multiple value-feelings. Unity only exists in the becoming of the multiple entities.

(2) Because of power symbols and representative manifestations of a society arising from the need for leadership, for defense, the desire for priority among nations, and demands of the common welfare, limits are inherent in the reasons of the society. The "aim" of society is different from that of the concrescence of the individual.

(3) What a society does in fact is what it is. Its operability is based on the value-feelings elicited by the intensity of the above-mentioned ethical factors. These value-feelings are expressed by symbols of unity. However, the symbols of unity must be exemplified by the functioning of the society. If they are not, the society is a fraud.

(4) The ethics and psychology of a society are interrelated in the psycho-historical process of its becoming a society. It is difficult to single out causes for success or failure. A society can only indicate its nature. Its operation, or the way it functions, will define its position in the civilizational spectrum.

(5) When a society fails to discern the pattern of its process, it remains stagnantly representative of the past. For example, when a society fails to be conscious of the fact that violence has become an accepted value in its pattern of activity and the "dynamic" of the pattern is labeled "peace," then awareness has either not had a proper or adequate response, or awareness of the problematic was not realized at all.

These suggestions are merely descriptive of the problematic of our social occasions. They point to a reconceptualization of the tools or concepts which Whitehead has offered us. An application of his thoughts concerning individual actual occasions must continually return to the modes of becoming which give these occasions life, i.e., the totality.

The reversibility of "society-individual" is also essential if the totality is to survive as a continual process returning again and again to the concrete. When one speaks of the society and its "common good," the acute danger is to leave the individuals behind. Herein lies the reality of the pitfalls of a socio-ethical psychology. Is it possible that this danger is unavoidable? If it is unavoidable we must then consider two modes of psycho-ethics—one mode for the individual (with all the ramifications of process theory) and another mode for the social unit utilizing the ramifications of process theory with the pretense (perhaps hope?) of universality. The ethical paradox gives us a novel context for the working out of the roles of both the self and the society in decision-making. The "limitation" value is built into the organic complex of life itself and so, too, is the potential for transcendence. While importance is the level of intensity of feeling and conviction attached to the paradigm or construct, transcendence is the ability to go beyond the paradigm and construct to reshape them in the light of a novel occasion.

If religion is a process of valuing, then it is also ethical in what it does. If religion speaks to the concrete facts of everyday issues then it must respond to the elusive discipline of bioethics. Bioethics comprises the paradoxical relationship of man as an individual confronting the environment of the physician, research scientist, geneticist, and consumer. In that environment the "I" quickly loses significance and is rendered operationally defunct, for neither the individual concerned nor the specialist has learned the value process of making important. A value ontology does not surround the quality of the relationship either directly or indirectly. Process thought, when applied to ethical-religious concerns, enables men to envision the I in the transient world, an I who makes something important ("valuable") by relating to it with intense interest. One has this attitude in the biomedical field, yet one experiences helplessness because the unprecedented information engages us in what Jacques Monod has termed "the ethics of knowledge."[44]

NOTES

1. Alfred North Whitehead, *Science and the Modern World*, (New York: Macmillan, 1953 [A Free Press Paperback, 1925]), pp. 191–192.

2. Cf. Alfred North Whitehead, *Religion in the Making* (Cleveland: World, 1960 [Meridian Books, 1966], originally published by Macmillan, 1926), pp. 87–91: See also *Process and Reality: An Essay in Cosmology* (New York: Harper Torchbooks, 1960, originally published by Macmillan, 1929), pp. 27, xix. Cf. R. W. Sperry, "Science and the Problem of Values," *Zygon* IX, no. 1 (March 1974), pp. 7–21; and Alfred E. Emerson and Ralph Wendell Burhoe, "Evolutionary Aspects of Freedom, Death, and Dignity," *Zygon* IX, no. 2 (June 1974), pp. 156–182.

3. Alfred North Whitehead, *Adventures of Ideas* (New York: Macmillan [Free Press Paperback], 1967, originally published in 1933 by Macmillan), p. 282.

4. *Process and Reality*, pp. 36, 320.

5. Ibid., p. 37. The categories of explanation (pp. 37–38) provide definitions for the happenings within the process of reality.

6. Cf. *Modes of Thought* (New York: Macmillan [a Free Press Paperback, 1968], 1938), "expression," pp. 20–41. Cf. Alfred North Whitehead, *Science and the Modern World*, p. 87. See also *Modes of Thought*, p. 174, and *Process and Reality*, pp. 15–16.

7. *Religion in the Making*, p. 89. *Science and the Modern World*, p. 125.

8. *Modes of Thought*, p. 119.

> Power is the compulsion of composition. The essence of power is the drive towards aesthetic worth for its own sake. All power is a derivative from this fact of composition attaining worth for itself. There is no other fact. Power and importance are aspects of this fact. It constitutes the drive of the universe. It is efficient cause, maintaining its power for survival. It is final cause, maintaining in the creature its appetition for creation.

Both of these moving forces—power and importance—are the qualities which render facts meaningful. Whitehead states further:

> Fact includes in its own nature something which is not fact, although it constitutes a realized item within fact. This is the conceptual side of fact. But, as usual, the philosophic tradition is too abstract. There is no such independent item in actuality as "mere concept." The concept is always clothed with emotion, that is to say, with hope or with fear, or with hatred, or with eager aspiration, or with the pleasure of analysis. The variations in the quality of appetition are infinite. But the notion of mere concept, or of mere realization, apart from the relevant emotional derivation, which is its emotional origin, is fallacious. (p. 122)

9. Ibid.

10. Ibid., p. 88. Ideal forms exist in relation to particular circumstances. They do, however, "carry over" as values or disvalues from previous individual and social prehending activities. Cf. *Science and the Modern World*, p. 159. In "Immortality" from *Essays in Science and Philosophy* (New York: Philosophical Library, Inc., 1947), pp. 79–80, Whitehead distinguishes between "the World of passing fact" and "the World of

Value." "The World which emphasizes Persistence is the World of Value. Value is in its mature timeless and immortal. Its essence is not rooted in any passing circumstance. The immediacy of some mortal circumstance is only valuable because it shares in the immortality of some value. The value inherent in the Universe has an essential independence of any moment of time; *and yet it loses its meaning apart from its necessary reference to the World of passing fact.* Value refers to Fact and Fact refers to Value" (emphasis mine). It seems to me that values (meaning here timeless, enduring truths) are *within* the finite. Possibility is the key here. I disagree, then, with the latter part of A. H. Johnson's statement in *Whitehead's Theory of Reality* (New York: Dover, 1962), p. 98: "Thus, it would seem that Whitehead is not offering two distinct theories of value. Rather, he is pointing out there *are value ideals* (abstract possibilities—eternal objects) which when realized or exemplified, constitute actual values." I would say actual values contain value ideals which when realized refer back to the antecedent standard.

11. *Modes of Thought*, p. 124.

12. Alfred North Whitehead, *The Function of Reason* (Boston: Beacon Press, 1967 [1929]), p. 20.

13. Ibid., p. 89. See also *Religion in the Making*, p. 101. Here Whitehead describes all order—even moral order—as aesthetic order which reflects a dual aspect of the function of the nature of God. "The actual world is the outcome of the aesthetic order, and the aesthetic order is derived from the immanence of God."

14. Cf. *The Function of Reason*, p. 23.

15. *Science and the Modern World*, p. 158.

16. Cf. ibid., p. 125. Whitehead describes endurance as "the repetition of the pattern in successive events."

17. Cf. "Immortality," from *Essays in Science and Philosophy*, pp. 84–85. Personal identity, involving "a sequence of actual occasions, each with its own present immediacy, is such that each occasion embodies in its own being the antecedent members of that sequence with an emphatic experience of the self-identity of the past in the immediacy of the present. This is the realization of personal identity."

18. Ibid., p. 88. "Values require each other. The essential character of the World of Value is coordination. Its activity consists in the approach to multiplicity by the adjustment of its many potentialities into finite unities, each unity with a group of dominant ideas of value, mutually interwoven, and reducing the infinity of values into a graduated perspective, fading into complete exclusion."

19. Cf. *Science and the Modern World*, p. 177.

20. Ibid., p. 178.

21. Ibid.

22. Ibid. In connection with this description of God, Whitehead refers to the issue at hand, i.e.,

> that what is metaphysically indeterminate has nevertheless to be categorically determinate. We have come to the limit of rationality. For there is a categorical limitation which does not spring from any metaphysical reason. There is a metaphysical need for a principle of determination, but there can be no metaphysical reason for what is

determined. If there were such a reason, there would be no need for any further principle: for metaphysics would already have provided the determination. The general principle of empiricism depends upon the doctrine that there is a principle of concretion which is not discoverable by abstract reason. What further can be known about God must be sought in the region of particular experience, and therefore rests on an empirical base.

Here the cultural factor in the entire epistemological setting (including mine) explored in the text finds its unique place.

23. A similar description of the relation of Zen Buddhism to the human situation is given by Richard DeMartino in "The Human Situation and Zen Buddhism," found in *Zen Buddhism and Psychoanalysis*, ed. D. T. Suzuki, Erich Fromm, and Richard DeMartino (New York: Grove Press, 1963).

24. *Religion in the Making*, pp. 92–93.

25. In *Modes of Thought*, p. 8, Whitehead defines importance as "interest, involving that intensity of individual feeling which leads to publicity of expression." But he states that this is inadequate because there are two aspects of importance—one based on unity of the universe and the other based on the individuality of the details. "Importance [just as the concept "value"] *leans* toward the former." Later in the same chapter, Whitehead aligns "importance" with that aspect of feeling whereby a perspective is imposed upon the universe of things felt," p. 11. Grades of effectiveness are imposed on things by the *functions* they fulfill for us.

26. See *Science and the Modern World*, pp. 161–162.

27. See *Religion in the Making*, p. 97.

> To be an actual entity is to have a self-interest. This self-interest is a feeling of self-valuation; it is an emotional tone. The value of other things, not one's self, is the derivative value of being elements contributing to this ultimate self-interest. This self-interest is the interest of what one's existence, as in that epochal occasion, comes to. It is the ultimate enjoyment of being actual.
>
> But the actuality is the enjoyment, and this enjoyment is the experiencing of value.

28. Ibid., p. 58.

29. Ibid., p. 100.

30. *Religion in the Making*, p. 59; cf. p. 120.

31. I have paraphrased an insight of Thomas White, my student at San Diego State University, regarding the nature of "the revelation of character."

32. *Religion in the Making*, p. 104.

33. Ibid., p. 104.

34. "Immortality," p. 90.

35. *Religion in the Making*, p. 152.

36. Ibid., pp. 151–152. See John Dewey's criticism of Alfred North Whitehead's philosophical method. Dewey refers to his method as either "genetic functionalism" or "functionalism." (See "genetic functionalism" in "Whitehead's Philosophy," *The Philosophical Review* XLVI, no. 2 [January 1927], pp. 170–177; read to the eastern division of the American Philosophical Association at the Symposium on Whitehead's Philosophy, December 29, 1926; and see "functionalism" in "The Philosophy of Whitehead," in

The Philosophy of Alfred North Whitehead.) See also Stephen Lee Ely's approach to Whitehead's God in *The Religious Availability of Whitehead's God: A Critical Analysis* (Madison: University of Wisconsin Press, 1942). Dorothy Emmet interprets Whitehead's God as "the necessary metaphysical ground of all possibilities whatever, both those actualized and those waiting for actualization, and, by reason of the Ontological Principle, Himself actual Being and not merely an ideal," in *Whitehead's Philosophy of Organism*, 2d ed. (New York: St. Martin's Press, 1932). For a summary of the nature of God see *Process and Reality*, pp. 521–533.

37. Alfred North Whitehead, "Mathematics and the Good," in *Essays in Science and Philosophy*, pp. 105–106; cf. *Religion in the Making*, pp. 145–146.

38. *Process and Reality*, p. 527. With regard to the consequent nature of God, Whitehead states:

> The wisdom of subjective aim prehends every actuality for what it can be in such a perfected system—its sufferings, its sorrows, its failures, its triumphs, immediacies of joy—woven by rightness of feeling into the harmony of the universal feeling, which is always immediate, always many, always one, always with novel advance, moving onward and never perishing. The revolts of destructive evil, purely self-regarding, are dismissed into their triviality of merely individual facts; and yet the good they did achieve in individual joy, in individual sorrow, in the introduction of needed contrast, is yet saved by its relation to the completed whole. (p. 525)

39. In *Process and Reality*, p. 34, Whitehead defines "ingression" as referring to the "particular mode in which the potentiality of an eternal object is realized in a particular actual entity, contributing to the definiteness of that actual entity."

40. "Immortality," pp. 79–80. See note 10.

> Value is the general category for the infinity of Values, partly concordant and partly discordant. The essence of these Values is their capacity for realization in the world of action. Such realization involves the exclusion of discordant values. Thus the World of Values must be conceived as active with the adjustment of potentialities for realization. This activity of internal adjustment is expressed by our moral and aesthetic judgments. (p. 80)

41. *Adventures of Ideas*, p. 270.

42. *Religion in the Making*, p. 127. Expression is the common manifestation of direct intuition by individual recipients. Intuition is most important here. Whitehead states that

> apart from such interpretation, the modes of expression remain accidental, unrationalized happenings of mere sense-experience; but with such interpretation, the recipient extends his apprehension of the ordered universe by penetrating into the inward nature of the originator of the expression. There is then a community of intuition by reason of the sacrament of expression proffered by one and received by the other.

Cf. Alfred North Whitehead, "Uses of Symbolism," in *Symbolism in Religion and Literature*, ed. with an introduction by Rollo May (New York: George Braziller, 1960), taken from Whitehead's *Symbolism: Its Meaning and Effect* (New York: Macmillan, 1927). Whitehead describes the function of symbols as giving definiteness, being manageable and reproducible and charged with emotional efficacy. This is a witness to the *importance* of the "functional feeling" (my term) of Whitehead's epistemology.

43. In *Modes of Thought*, p. 109, Whitehead states emphatically,

> Everything has some value for itself, for others, and for the whole. This characterizes the meaning of actuality. By reason of this character, constituting reality, the conception of morals arises. We have no right to deface the value experience which is the very essence of the universe. Existence, in its own nature, is the upholding value intensity. Also no unit can separate itself from the others, and from the whole. And each unit exists in its own right. It upholds value intensity for itself, and this involves sharing value intensity with the universe. Everything that in any sense exists has two sides, namely, its individual self and its signification in the universe. Also either of these aspects is a factor in the other.

44. Cf. Jacques Monod, "On the Logical Relationship between Knowledge and Values," in *The Biological Revolution: Social Good or Social Evil*, ed. Watson Fuller, cited in Chapter IV, note 2.

IV

Reshaping the "Religious" toward Bioethics and Abortion

I take the position that the science of survival must be built on the science of biology and enlarged beyond the traditional boundaries to include the most essential elements of the social sciences and the humanities with emphasis on philosophy in the strict sense, meaning "love of wisdom." A science of survival must be more than science alone, and I, therefore, propose the term *Bioethics* in order to emphasize the two most important ingredients in achieving the new wisdom that is so desperately needed: biological knowledge and human values.[1]

The problematic of decision-making in the complex of the individual, the personal, and the social is most keenly felt in what is coming to be known as the discipline of bioethics. Bioethics is concerned with establishing ethical guidelines through ethical and moral levels of discourse for the meeting of the life sciences and the conduct of human affairs, individually, personally, and socially. The lack of precedent for the formulation of vitally novel constructs from traditional paradigms is bewildering to medical, theological, and religiously oriented personnel. The advances of a technological society involve a binding together of research and ethical reflection. An "ethics of knowledge" requires normative values.[2] I would concur with the guidelines Dr. Callahan has outlined in his essay "Bioethics as a Discipine." He speaks of three tasks for the bioethicist: "definition of issues, methodological strategies, and procedures for decision-making."[3] The paradox of decision-making confronts us in the realization that the ones who will make the day-to-day practical decisions are the physicians and the biologists who are not trained in philosophical discourse while it falls to the philosophers and the theologians to discover the methodological strategies and procedural criteria.[4]

The criteria Dr. Callahan outlines for a sound methodology suggest that bioethics be truly interdisciplinary as well as enabling "those who employ it to reach reasonably specific, clear decisions in those instances which require them."[5] Service to the practitioners is of paramount importance. But part of the methodological concern demands the interaction of many issues exposed by the life sciences. The ethician may serve to provide

> sociological understanding of the kinds of needs felt by researchers and clinicians, patients and physicians, and the varieties of pressures to which they are subject; historical understanding of the sources of regnant value theories and common practices; requisite scientific training; awareness of and facility with the usual methods of ethical analysis as understood in the philosophical and theological communities—and no less a full awareness of the limitations of those methods when applied to actual cases; and, finally, personal exposure to the kinds of ethical problems which arise in medicine and biology.[6]

The controversy over what bioethics should be concerned with is by no means settled by this outline. Paul Ramsey, for example, is of the opinion that "it is not a matter of settling the *procedures* for deciding difficult medico-moral issues. The error of thinking in terms of decision-making models is the special temptation of a professional ethics in a relativistic age and in a pluralistic culture."[7] Nor does he agree with Robert Veatch's suggestion of a universal ethic.[8] Professor Ramsey's concern is with the "what" of ethics—away from the decisional procedures "to the features of attitude and actions that make them right, and to principles of ethical appraisal."[9] He therefore suggests the broad outlines of a normative medical ethics beginning with the "ultimate requirement or standard or warrant," care.

> "Care" has the advantage of locating medical ethics within the ethics of a wider human community. It also locates our model

for medical decision-making alongside other models: Jewish ethics whose ultimate norm is *hesed* or steadfast fidelity to the covenant of life and Christian ethics whose final appeal and criteria of judgment are Christian love and compassion. Religious ethics would be inclined to ascribe "sanctity" to human life and call for more than "care" and "respect" for life. We need not go into that, since "care" can be understood in a strong sense and may blend in one degree or another with those other sources of judgment. Medical ethics, we can minimally say within an editorial in *California Medicine,* has "had the blessing of the Judeo-Christian tradition," but we need not be concerned with the interconnections between medical ethics and other models of normative decision-making.[10]

This position is most interesting and follows the path of reasoning which I have discussed concerning the separation of the spiritual function of theology and religious ethics. What Professor Ramsey is doing is applying the concept "care" to the rules of practice, principles of actions, and "covenants of loyalty" (moral institutions) when relating to the dignity of patients and research subjects. However, the concept "care" seems to be a compromise which doesn't quite come up to the function of morality. Further, the dilemma over different social and medical priorities is also a stumbling block to "care" as a norm especially when the inequities of life are so blatant as to demand at every level a reordering of concepts in the cultural spectrum to test its validity.[11] I believe that a concept chosen as an ultimate principle because it suggests the personal quality of human life is insufficient to handle complex multidimensional questions and the paradoxes of the life sciences.

Dr. Leon Kass approaches the question of the new biology from the perspective of the needs to which it responds and the limits which it offers in a structure suggesting the parameters of an ontology. He acknowledges that the use of techniques, whether scientific or not, always involves moral and political issues. "All private or public decisions to develop or use biomedical technology—and decisions not to do so—inevitably contain judgments about value. This is true even if the values guiding those decisions are not articulated or made clear, as indeed they often are not."[12] He further agrees with Dr. Callahan and others who suggest that they cannot be derived from biomedical science. The point I wish to emphasize is that their point of derivation is not so important as the way in which they are appropriated to other dimensions of existence. Professor Ramsey's rationale is a compromise but it maintains an ultimate goal and that is what *spirituality* is about, not religion and certainly not ethics. Dr. Kass also suggests the limitations, rather than simply the exceptions to his rationale. First, men control science and therefore nature. Second, someone is always deciding even when it appears that no one is making a decision. Concern for money, success, and power affects the use of biomedical technologies, research, and the future of any project. Thus, at a social level, benefits and risks in the economics of the institution are weighed carefully in judgments about values. However, to save the lives of many individuals, considerations other than what are benefits and risks at the institutional level may be necessary. Society does not offer us a consistent image of what it is ethics ought to be about.

> The very pragmatism that makes us sensitive to considerations of economic cost often blinds us to larger social costs exacted by biomedical advances. For one thing, we seem to be unaware that we may not be able to maximize all the benefits, that several of the goals we are promoting conflict with each other. On the one hand, we seek to control population growth by lowering fertility; on the other hand we develop techniques to enable every infertile woman to bear a child. On the one hand, we try to extend the lives of individuals with genetic disease; on the other, we wish to eliminate deleterious genes from the human population.[13]

The problematic is further complicated when the technique of how is coupled with the philosophy of "why" and "why not." Underlying assumptions about the nature of life and sustenance, life and progress, life and values, creep into what decision-makers themselves believe about these issues. For this reason, constructs which serve the purpose of operable functions within the parameters of the ontology of the issue debated or discussed are of paramount importance. Although relativity must enter into the considerations, relativity is not the criterion upon which to build a human focus. Professor Ramsey is correct in his claim that cultural pluralism is simply inadequate as an indicator of multiple ethical images. The paradox of the individual and social needs and constraints is something else. Recognition of the core of the problematic facing the ethician simply points to its division into workable dimensions. What may be defined as "care" at one level may be defined as insensitivity at another. Motivations for actions are contingent upon the priority of the issue for one element of the society or another. The discipline of bioethics is most important since it focuses on the normative qualities of both the obvious and the hidden dimensions of the issue.

An ethician is involved in the "complex science" of analyzing ethical argumentation.[14]

> A good ethicist should be able to show how, beginning with any particular normative theory and weighing principles, etc., one *might* reach a particular reading of the moral data. In this regard he is like the philosopher of science who describes how one might make a particular (nonmoral) scientific observation based upon a given set of assumptions about the nature of reality. He is like the skilled psycho-physiologist who had a well developed theory of color perception.[15]

This does not mean that he will be better in his evaluation or judgment in the last analysis. It does mean that he will be able to interpret the information to discover possible readings, and therefore possible options, in the decision-making process. He may well be able to entertain creatively new constructs of operability and he will definitely be able to highlight the important benefits and limitations intrinsic to the ethical value of the options. We do not yet have a person who is trained to be an ethician with the theoretical tools of the trade.[16] But, it is precisely this area of intellectual and practical expertise which demands the training comparable to that of any facet of the medical profession. Without the sound expression of the reshaping of paradigms which have dictated to morality, to the medical model, and to our broad cultural values, there can be no adequate handling of the issues at all. Bioethics as a discipline must be creative in its venture, and serve those who make decisions by analysis of data and assessment of possibilities. Just as scientific research utilizes experimentation so, too, the bioethician must be willing to experiment with viable concepts to prove them to be operable constructs in the realm of decision-making, never forgetting for one instant that man is limited by the fact that he can make decisions. This is his opportunity to stop the process of life by grasping one moment. Thus, the freedom which the ethician may create will be his very limitation. But, as Charles Hartshorne has put it, "I heartily support the search for a better system of risk-opportunity, more appropriate to our technology than we have now."[17]

Evidence of "risk-taking opportunity" is found in the initial recommendation of Senator Walter F. Mondale and the subsequent Senate Joint Resolution 145 establishing a National Commission on Health Science and Society (1968). As proposed by Senator Mondale, the commission would "study the meaning of health science research and development for this nation and the world, explore its moral and ethical implications and formulate ethical guidelines for its application and make recommendations to the President and Congress for actions to assure that our social policies reflect and influence our technological advances."[18] With the adoption of this resolution the Institute of Society, Ethics, and the Life Sciences was founded and is under the direction of Dr. Daniel Callahan, a philosopher of religion.[19] Additions to this initial resolution have come in the form of the establishment of a national program of biomedical research fellowships, traineeships and training to assure continued excellence of biomedical research.[20] Further, a commission was established to "undertake a comprehensive investigation and study to identify the basic ethical principles and develop guidelines which should underlie the conduct of biomedical and behavioral research involving human subjects and develop and implement policies and regulations to assure that such research is carried out in accordance with the ethical principles identified by the Commission in order to assure the full protection of the rights of the subjects of such research."[21]

The ethical implications of biomedical research is the concern of the professional ethician who can creatively and ably entertain the "risk-taking opportunity." But it must not stop at that. Only when the material is filtered down through the educational process to those for whom the research is being conducted will the fruits of the work be accomplished. Dr. Lederberg stresses,

> The entire purpose of scientific research is publication, making new knowledge available to the entire scientific community. And you do not have to be the person who has discovered some new facet of the scientific information in the laboratory to be necessarily the best person to interpret this to the rest of the community. The process of publication in the scientific literature insures the free availability of this knowledge, and it is often the case that the man who is thoroughly preoccupied with advancing the frontier really does not have time to do that, and at the same time do the synthesis, the generalization, and the communication which is so important for our social purposes.[22]

The teaching of bioethics by ethicians can be a way of testing the quality of the information and of insuring the communication of biomedical advances to the consumer.

At the hearings to establish the Commission on Health, Science, and Society a significant question was raised by Dr. Kenneth Vaux, professor of ethics at the Institute of Religion and Human Development, Texas Medical Center, Houston, Texas.

> If we decide to continue to control and restructure man through the full range of means at our disposal (surgical, biomedical, psychological, sociological, technological), what in man is it proper to change, restructure and alter? When we speak of the divinely endowed dignity of man, are there dimensions of man's humanity which are inviolable and should not be transgressed?[23]

It is to this question, the inevitable question, that we come in search of the justifiable and the normative amid biomedical research. Technique may steer a course of indifference to the traditional values men have perceived. For this reason, the important paradigms of Western man cannot simply be ignored without creating upheaval in the psychological sphere of his individual and social life. The epistemological parameters which I have outlined direct the insights of life's process toward factual data of raw experience while they maintain the independent value of memory, forgetfulness, and imagination—including importance and transcendence. The ethician can only construct operable hypotheses if the appeal is made to the holistic sensitivity which an individual possesses as a social and therefore potentially personal being.

One of the functions of religion in our way of life has been to provide the security that all will be well and that progress will be rewarded through sacrifice and self-denial. Concern for others has sometimes, but not always, motivated that essential movement—progress. Progress is an example of a construct which has proceeded from a demythologized and extrapolated biblical view of history. Progress, derived from a linear view of cosmic and human direction, has been immortalized as an ultimate value. Professor Roger L. Shinn has referred to progress as a "secularization of the biblical view of history."

> The Hebrews broke with the great cosmological myth, characteristic of most ancient cultures, that intercepted history according to the cyclical pattern of nature. They saw a linear, purposive history, moving toward a messianic age. They were not progressivist; they saw the precariousness of life and they were sensitive to human frailty and sin. Belief in redemption through suffering and grace is not the same thing as belief in progress. But they believed that history, the doing of God and men, had a direction.[24]

When the messianic hope turned otherworldly, this dynamic sense of history disappeared for a time. According to Professor Shinn, two major impulses reproduced faith in progress—the Enlightenment and the theory of evolution. The context of progress has expanded today to include biomedical advances. This kind of progress forces a blending of the dynamic sense of history and a reverence for the mediational values between this world and the next, a blending not easily accomplished. Just as Christianity lost its way through the hope of messianism, it is now in danger of avoiding the "risk-taking opportunities" in favor of either more esoteric forms of transcendence or a return to "biblical essentials." This means ignoring the course of history, the adequacy of human intention, and loss of faith in the cosmic process. Factors such as *"what one believes about the human condition"* and about the destiny of progress are truly the motivational necessities that control and determine decision-making.[25] The relocation of priorities and the reshaping of self-images of human perfection have more influence in the name of progress than scientific facts, legal arguments, and technocratic know-how. The phenomenology of making important is crucial to the reshaping of values.

Within the framework of the individual, models of self-sacrifice, self-denial and concern for others are rather easy to supply. But what of unprecedented issues which perplex the medical personnel and the biologists and force the theologians to surface the moral wisdom of the past? Religion cannot be identical with the spirituality of the past. If religion is to meet the dilemmas of our technocracy it must not simply assume that religion has only been a form of "personal knowledge," a type of spirituality, i.e., elevation and salvation of the soul.[26] Leaders such as Confucius, Jesus, Buddha, Lao-Tzu, have been mediators between self-mastery and world-consciousness without whom man could not meaningfully order his life. Such innovators have established mediational truths. Religion must not deny the spiritual, mediational roles of holy men, prophets, and reformers. They assure us by their sensitivity to the human dimension as well as to the transcendent dimensions of which we may not be aware. Religion must translate supernaturalism into an immanent concern for the world in which we live, and leave the spiritual concern to the vertical dimension. Finally, religion must reshape the wisdom of the ages into operable suggestions for the inviobility of "nature," "life," "death," "human being," "self," and other pertinent concepts which become key constructs in man's thinking and behavior. These suggestions, however, should not be permanent in their descriptive quality. Change and its consequences are to be allowed if a process perspective is maintained. Religion must be reshaped into a holistic concern for the total man in the world. This concern is demanded by the relativity of a culture to which we owe a legacy for the future. Within this process of reconstruction and reshaping, religion forces upon man the realization of limitation. Much of life defies self-mastery, self-discipline, and control.

In view of the focus of religion on the ethical, it is imperative that the religious ethician has the task of suggesting constructs. The religious ethician has at his disposal the wealth of the world's systems of belief which offer, in many instances, an operable wisdom which has gone unnoticed. While I have questioned the traditional morality of Western Christianity because of the urgency of our ethical situation, I have not discarded its potential for the reshaping of the paradigms as well as the images of the healing process.

In the light, however, of the academic study of religion as a quasi-scientific endeavor, I believe that a comparative approach to religion may allow us to extrapolate many of the concepts which Eastern religion has utilized in understanding the process of self-consciousness and the process of life itself. It is difficult to separate the dimensions of Eastern religious thought into doctrine, morality, practice, etc. Because of the nature of the process of the world and the place of the self in that process, man is one. An example of a religious paradigm which suggests this processive nature of all things is Buddhism in the meaning of Siddhartha Gautama's classical message. It is not the message or the man which I emphasize, but the character of importance, the intensity of feeling and cognitive reason which is attached to the truth about the world which is of interest. The incorporation of the sophisticated psychological experience of Buddhism as a tradition encompassing a deep reverence for the mediational character of religious truths of all faiths—including ethical and spiritual concerns—may become part of the reshaping process I am suggesting. What follows is an effort to point out the affinities for an operational process which Buddhism contains.

Religion, as defined by Clifford Geertz (see the Introduction), refers to the distinctive traditions of the world as they exist independent of each other. I maintain, however, that independent existence may serve spiritual functions but it does not serve the ethical demands of our time. For example, Christianity is hard put to find biblical and theological precedents for biomedical concerns. Often theologians return to the universal truths and pump them until they have created a response to the issue. Love is a perfect example of universal truth which becomes both the motivation and the goal for Christians of whatever denomination, sect, or tradition. In the face of knowledge of psychiatry and psychology concerning the intimate relationship between conditioning, the emotions, such as trust, fear, and love, and the will, love still remains unquestionably the priority. The model is "Love thy neighbor as thyself" even when people do not know how to love either themselves or their neighbor.[27] Despite Freud's astute observation which has been enlarged and expanded upon by contemporary theorists, the love principle is still offered as operable in all things. With Reinhold Niebuhr, I suggest love is a goal and not the motivational force it appears to be in religious paradigms. In the face of this, how then does one proceed to assess one's motivational factors? I suggest that love be recast in a setting conducive to its lasting importance. Place "love" within a deliberate understanding of the total complex of the human situation. Place it in the realm of the defenseless ego. Equip that ego with choice. Attend to the composite feelings of fear, anger, hate, and trust. In that context, open up a relational focus—love whom? Love them becomes a "construct."

The insight of the Buddhist philosophy of life begins with the honest truth of man's "self" position. The self "desires," "thirsts," "craves" something more, less, other. The motivational framework of suffering (grounded in ignorance, [*avidyā*]) is the beginning of the sense of self which is also the beginning of the end of self. The goal and process of *śūnyatā* (emptiness) is the perception that personality contains nothing that really belongs to it. *Śūnyatā* suggests the dialectical nature of reality and the coincidence of two opposite aspects of the ontological structure of the self.[28] (It is swollen [*śūnya*] with something that is not itself, and at the same time is itself.) The nature of the self and reality is conveyed by the concept "Suchness." "One takes reality such as it is, without superimposing any ideas upon it."[29] *Śūnyatā* and Suchness are one in that the process of emptying oneself of self is the process

87

of taking things as they are in the cosmological process of life and death.

The basis of Buddhist thought is a process principle. "All is impermanence." All things are subject to change and therefore conditioned to a process of becoming. Further, the law of *karma* operates in such a way that man is what he does. "The Buddhist who knows Buddhism will reply that this law of universal impermanence, which has been preached by the founder of his religion, is inseparably connected with the law of cause and effect, for nothing in this phenomenal world can exist without some causes while the very name *phenomenon* presupposes origination, which again implies destruction, exactly in the same way as destruction invariably implies origination."[30] The principle of process and its link to cause and effect is described in two forms in Buddhist thought: (a) the Four Noble Truths and (b) the Chain of Causation linking together the twelve preconditions of the life process. Both forms presuppose the principle of suffering as an inevitable consequence of change and transition. Suffering becomes an ontological principle of existence. The Four Noble Truths consist of the following: (1) the recognition that there is suffering (*dukkha*). Suffering is an off-centeredness, unrest, physical and mental commotion, disease, pain or ill. (2) Suffering has a cause. This cause is specifically identified as a "thirst," "craving," or "desire." (3) Since suffering has a cause, it can be extinguished by getting rid of the cause. (4) The Way (path) to extinguish suffering is the Eightfold Path. The Eightfold Path is qualified by the concept "right," which in the context of "adequate" represents a construct operable for the purposes outlined above. If intentions or motivations should not prove to be adequate to one's purposes, then the action, thought, and conduct of the individual would not be "right." A reordering of intentional priorities in line with the goals would be necessary. Thus, the modification of understanding, aspiration, speech and conduct, livelihood, effort, recollection and *samadhi* (tranquility, i.e., "the transcending of empirical consciousness") by "right" indicates not merely an effort but an attitudinal perspective.[31]

Within the scope of the problematic of human existence, Buddhism suggests that because the uncertainty of life, self, and conditional things cause unrest, the only perception in which the healing process can take place is a "right" one. This "fittingness" or "adequacy" is close to a de-ontological perspective—paradoxically within an ontological framework. "A de-ontologist contends that it is possible for an action or rule of action to be morally right or obligatory even if it does not promote the greatest possible balance of good over evil for self, society, or universe. It may be right or obligatory simply because of some other fact about it or because of its own nature."[32]

The second form consists of the twelve preconditions understood in a chain moving backward (the precondition itself is underlined):

(12) *aging and dying* depend on birth (if there were no birth, then there would be no death);

(11) *birth* depends on becoming (if life x did not die and come to be life y, then there would be no birth of y);

(10) *becoming* depends on appropriation (if the life process did not appropriate phenomenal materials just as fire appropriates fuel, then there would be nontransmigration);

(9) *appropriation* depends on craving (if one did not thirst for sense objects, for coming to be, after this life, and for ceasing to be after this life, then the transmigration process would not appropriate fuel);

(8) *craving* depends on feeling (if pleasant and painful feelings were not experienced, then one would be conditioned to seek continuing experience of the pleasant or cessation of the unpleasant);

(7) *feeling* depends on contact (the meeting of sense and object is necessary before pleasure or pain can be felt);

(6) *contact* depends on the six sense fields (the six pairs of sense and datum);

(5) *the six sense fields* depend on name-and-form (mind and body; as the sense fields are equivalent to name-and-form, some lists of the preconditions omit the sense field);

(4) *name-and-form*, the whole living organism depends on consciousness, which here means the spark of sentient life that enters the womb and animates the embryo;

(3) *consciousness* depends on the dispositions accrued throughout life as karmic residues of deeds, words, and thoughts;

(2) and the *karmic legacy* that produces rebirth depends on ignorance of the Four Holy Truths;

(1) *ignorance.*

The relation between the links is implication. As a theory of causation, this "dependent arising" concerns the formal concomitances between things rather than their material derivation from one another. It resembles a medical diagnosis in several ways. By showing that the ailment depends on a series of conditions, it indicates the point at which the series can be broken and so facilitates a cure. This counteracts the theory that the disease is a fortuitous happening, against which no remedy would be effective, and also opposes the view that the ultimate cause of the malady is some entity outside the process, such as God or an immutable soul. Salvation from transmigration is to be found in the process of transmigration itself.[33]

The consequences of this phenomenological description are to offer us a perceptual option to our present Christian perspective. Translating the Buddhist philosophy into biomedical issues is to suggest: (1) that the questions of life and death are inevitable—not rewards or punishments—but real happenings which may be enhanced or depreciated by the attitude with which we approach (a) the process of life and death and (b) our self-concept in the process of life and death. (2) The evaluation by decision-making of one stage or another will affect what happens in the next moment(s). While that is irreversible, due to the permanence of suffering, the desire or craving to continue to change is important and ever present due to the structure of the ego. (3) Perfection as an idealistic image of man's static nature does not exist. Neither universal creation nor an individual object soul exists.

A recent article by Alfred E. Emerson and Ralph Wendell Burhoe expresses diversity as the priority within unity and not vice versa.[34] A *premature* perfection (my emphasis) is too idealistic to accomplish an ethical understanding of what is in process.

> Perfection . . . does not allow for any dysfunction, disequilibrium, differentials, variation, struggle, competition, pain, suffer-

ing, disease, sacrifice, death, or evil in any sort of biological or human existence.[35]

This is precisely the problematic of the incompatibility of the idea of progress and the redemptive process. The paradox leans toward the elimination of the negative. The negative cannot be eliminated because man does not really choose to eliminate it. The research impulse creates freedom and limitation also. The grasping for the nonexistent can be dangerous and can lead to "destructive frustration."

> Diversity within unity is possible, but both are necessary aspects of life and cannot be fundamentally and sharply separated. Diversity and change produce the energy and matter that may later find ordered relations. The most basic scientific constants of which we are aware are formulae of relationships among differences. Relations are just as important as are the perceptions that are related. Unity is a relationship, but is inconceivable to us without diversity to unite.[36]

If perfection is a consciousness of the actuality of diversity then imperfection is a premature state of static endurance.

The purpose of the foregoing has been to prepare for a discussion of what is labeled "abortion." Abortion offers us an example of an unsolved dilemma for which we have few operable constructs within reshaped paradigms. I believe that the use of the epistemological parameters and the incorporation of a sense of life and death from the Buddhist perspective may offer us some insight first, into the paradox of the issue itself, and second, into some avenues of thought which may be pursued to reshape our thinking on the issue itself. Abortion as a religious ethical problem exposes us to the typical models and concepts which form the basis of decision-making in many of the other biomedical issues, such as the right to death with dignity. It is my contention that the existing concepts and models are inadequate to the issue because (1) they cannot be translated into operable constructs; (2) they do not issue forth from a perspective of processive change, imperfection, limitation, and the acceptance of life and death; (3) conditions which influence decision-making, such as the psychological well-being, the economic status, and the desire of the mother, are erroneously seen as the primary issues. In fact, the issue of the status of the conceptus as it develops in the process of life and death is *the* ethical reevaluation of the moral position that is involved.[37]

Life must be considered a continuous and dynamic process. Like the Buddhist conception, life is a cyclical process punctuated by birth and death. "While a cycle has no beginning, and paradoxical as it may seem, the cycle of life may be taken to begin with the creation of sperm and ova, which join to make a new being, who in turn may reach puberty and create sperms or ova, and the cycle goes on endlessly."[38] This processive view is viewed generationally by Professor Malcolm Potts:

> There is no single event marking the beginning of life, there is no Rubicon to be crossed during embryological development upon which we can concentrate and say, "Before this moment we have an object as trivial as a nailparing; after this time we have individual human being to which we must reserve the full sanctity of human life." An ethical system founded on biology must begin by recognizing that reproduction is a continuum which can be traced back to the time when the primordial germ cells are first recognizable in the yolk sac endoderm (at about the twentieth day after fertilization in man) and it is still incomplete when a grandmother babysits for her daughter's children.[39]

Recently *Time* magazine ran an article explaining the latest progress in the area of understanding the process of intrauterine photography.[40] Dr. Motoyuki Hayashi, chairman of the Department of Obstetrics and Gynecology at Tokyo's Toho University School of Medicine, using a culdoscope, filmed sequences of fetal development from inside the uterus of a woman scheduled to undergo an abortion for medical reasons. Apart from the ethical issue of allowing a pregnancy to continue for experimental purposes, later to be terminated, the process makes visible for us through a series of photographs definite stages of development. One is able to compare visually the ethical distinctions with one's sense of sight in the context of the process itself. I am not suggesting that simply the sight of a fetus at six weeks is an emotional experience conducive to the thwarting of an abortion. I

am saying that the whole process may be understood by the lay-
man when the mystique has been removed. The mystique which
surrounds pregnancy is due to sexual misinformation, ignorance,
lack of proper sex educaiton, our cultural conditioning, and
much more. But these issues cannot hide the process of development which we are appraising. The coupling of the cognitive
process with the senses contributes to more viable constructs in
ethical discourse. The mystique carries the weight of psychological
guilt, religious sinfulness, existential aloneness, and collective
unwantedness. However, the paradox is that in spite of these
effects, produced after the abortion (in many but not all cases),
the sense of lostness, abandonment, and righteousness experienced
before the abortion has the same effect, that is, an uneasiness about
the fundamental issue of the origin of life. That is the real mystique. There is confusion in the process of decision-making. To
make the decision is difficult; to live with the decision is just as
difficult.

Accompanying the sequence of photographs was a description
of the process itself.

> Magnified thousands of times, the beginnings of the process of
> conception looks like a volcano erupting as the ovary swells,
> ejects fluid and cells and, finally a mature egg. Drawn in by
> fingerlike projections called fimbria, the egg moves through the
> fallopian tube, which links the ovary to the uterus; the trip,
> which covers some five inches, takes from five to seven days.
> Developing in the male testicle, the precursors of sperm get
> ready to begin their journey to the egg; mature sperm, their
> black tails parallel, must make an upstream swim of less than
> a foot, an ordeal that can take anywhere from a few minutes to
> hours and one that only the strongest will complete.
> In the fallopian tube, sperm surround the egg in a dance of
> life. Smashing against the egg in their efforts to pierce its pro-
> tective covering, they always set it spinning counterclockwise.
> Once a single sperm has penetrated the egg, a chemical change
> takes place that keeps others from entering. Fertilized, the egg
> begins to divide, splitting first into two cells, then into four.
> By the time the fertilized egg reaches the uterus at the end of
> its week-long excursion, it has developed into a blastocyst, a
> ball of cells.
> Embedded in the wall of the uterus, the cluster of cells grows

rapidly; an organ such as the heart begins to form. After two months, the fetal spine can be discerned. By the end of the tenth week, the egg and the sperm have already been transformed into a complex and human-looking organism.[41]

The blastocyst may be spontaneously aborted and about 25 percent of them are. It is only after approximately the eighth week that the embryo is called a fetus. The construct "fetus" indicates that the organs are beginning to differentiate themselves. This, then, is the activity which is known as pregnancy and which, as a creative experience, demands the attendant emotions and cognitive attitude conducive to a responsive value toward the formation of new life. Without the attendant decision to accept the life which is possible as a result of the process, the process is unrelated to the lives of the mother and father out of which it develops. That relationship creates, as Professor Fontinell cited, the locus of possibility for personal growth. There can be no personal quality without a social relatedness. The decision is that of the individual. Without the freedom to make that decision, the act will have one or more residual effects to void the decision.

Within the process of decision-making regarding abortion, more than the process itself is at stake. The unique qualities of each phase will suggest ethical distinctions in the decision-making process. The issue of abortion must be seen not as one issue but rather as a complex of issues separated by the time and condition of the context in which the abortion is discussed. To "construct" a normative framework for the issue will alleviate the paradox and the peril of thought, feeling, and will of the woman and man to whom this might be a possibility. It is this task bioethics has as its revered trust. It is this qualitative approach to the quantitative process which gives a religious dimension to the binding together of man and the creative process. Seeking normative values, bioethics must not only consider the process, but the surrounding conditions in which and through which the process is unfolding. For example, has the mother been diagnosed to have a genetically defective fetus with a terminal illness such as cystic fibrosis? What are the motives for the abortion at each stage? Is the mother in physical danger? In what instances will the psychological health of the mother weigh more than the continuation of the organic process of pregnancy? These are some of the questions which form part of the conditions one must assess in the decision-making process. However, they must be assessed in the context of the stage of fetal development. The task of bioethics and abortion must focus on the organic complexity of pregnancy, beginning with the state of the embryo and the fetus.

To some, however, the issue of abortion has been removed from the theoretical—philosophical and religious—concerns into the practical locus of public health care. A recent review of *Abortion and Social Justice*[42] articulates the parameters of contemporary interest in the issue of abortion. Mr. Facione, the reviewer, begins by articulating a rather clinical perspective presently reflected, for example, in the political fabric of federal health funding:

> There is no longer an "abortion debate" going on across our country. Abortion, like violence and civil disobedience, has about run its course as a "live" issue in contemporary thought. This is not because the issue has been intellectually resolved; rather, the contrary is true, it has come to be seen as intellectually unresolvable. The attention of people has shifted away from the theoretical matters of whether and in what cases, if at all, an abortion is morally permissable, to the practical issues.[43]

True, the practical concerns of services, adequate financing, and population control are important, but they presuppose a closed theoretical issue of the ontological status of the fetus.

In the same article, the abortion debate is reopened as an "ethical theoretic" (my term), thus structuring the polar parameters of our issue.

> Many philosophical issues emerged or returned to prominence because of the abortion debate. Some of these questions may be framed as follows: 1) Given that the fetus is human, and even human life, in what sense, if any, can we say that it is a human individual, or a human person? 2) In what ways does it enjoy a claim to, or "right" to life? Does such a right result from the civil law, the natural law, the fetus' being human, its being an individual, its being a person, its having certain potentialities, its having certain levels of self-awareness of self-control, its potentiality having certain expressible or non-expressible desires,

or what? 3) In what ways is it necessary, desirable, undesirable, impossible, important, or unimportant to connect one's philosophical and religious views with public policy and civil law?[44]

Both poles—the practical and the theoretical—need operational goals and methods. Ethical theoretics can be instrumental in the functioning of the concrete issues if a relatedness is established between how the the theoretical positions are formulated and the limitation imposed by practical living at the individual and sociocultural levels.

Three elements are missing from Mr. Facione's review in the context of a radical questioning of the grounds of human reflection: (1) a method for separating individual concerns from the social, political, and legal areas of the abortion issue, as well as a method for the decision-making entailed in the evaluation process itself; (2) the dismissal of the erroneous assumption that we can ethically relate to a problem on one dimension alone, and further that consistency is the first rule. (3) On the contrary, multidimensionality involves a maintenance of continuity and development rather than consistency and must, by virtue of the facts of our national social psychology, be the direction an operational perspective takes.

The multidimensional approach to the issue does reveal certain paradoxes within each dimension and in instances of one dimension facing another. One example which has caused much controversy is the legal dimension. The legal perspective effecting public policy on decision-making in potential abortion cases can be found in the United States' Supreme Court cases Roe vs. Wade,[45] and Doe vs. Bolton.[46] On the basis of the external appraisal of fetal development, the Court decided that:

> For the stage prior to approximately the end of the first trimester, the abortion decision and its effectuation must be left to the medical judgment of the pregnant woman's attending physician. For the stage subsequent to approximately the end of the first semester, the State, in promoting its interest in the health of the mother, may if it chooses, regulate the abortion procedure in ways that are reasonably related to maternal health. For the stage subsequent to viability, the State, in promoting its interest in the potentiality of human life, may, if it chooses, regu-

late and even proscribe, abortion except where it is necessary, in appropriate medical judgment, for the preservation of the life or health of the mother.[47]

Within the last year abortion hearings by the Senate Judiciary Constitutional Amendments Subcommittee convened to hear testimony for and against the two proposed amendments guaranteeing the "right to life" of the unborn. If passed, these amendments would negate the January 22, 1973, Supreme Court decision. Senate Joint Resolution 119, proposed by James L. Buckley, "would give the constitutional right to the unborn except when 'reasonable medical certainty exists that continuation of the pregnancy will cause the death of the mother.' "[48] Senate Joint Resolution 130, proposed by Jesse A. Helms, "would give the right to life to all human beings from the moment of conception without exception."[49] The abortion debate continues with objections coming most strongly from Roman Catholic ecclesial authorities and laity.[50] Such phrases as "the right to life" are proferred as the religious and humanistic arguments against the Supreme Court decision. Other important considerations are the related issues of: (1) is abortion a legal issue at all? and (2) if religious influence changed the decision directly or indirectly, would that violate the first amendment to the Constitution as well as the basic principle of the separation of church and state? The deeper concern, the basic disposition or attitude regarding the viability of moral principles themselves, is at stake. Ethics must examine moral principles after a review of their operability. Religion is important here as well. The academic and scientific study of religion has revealed that dogmatic assertions about the nature of man and God are *decided* by many factors other than the intrinsic worth of the concept. Traditional religion also neglects the cultural conditioning of the psychological influences as well as the historical perspectives of many moral positions. In a word, the operational needs which may be met by a pro-abortion decision are not acknowledged to be real needs.

A further emphasis is the element of an imperative rather than choice. Decision-making, if based on imperatives, is not a free process. Such decision-making is usually based on the religious paradigm. Within the Roman Catholic tradition, the argument against abortion comes from the creation paradigm. Man is to repeat the creative pattern after the manner of God's order to Adam and Eve—Be fruitful and multiply and subdue the earth. God made man in his image; hence God is conceived as personal and anthropocentric. Man is subject to God alone. Therefore only God has the right to take life. Terminating an embryo or a fetus at any stage of development usurps the power reserved to God alone and terminates a potential life. It assumes that man is not the creator of his destiny in areas which simulate the creation paradigm. This position, while it is normative, is inflexible. While the creation paradigm offers responses of value to the questions of what is the "right to life"; what is the "sanctity of life"; more importantly, what is life itself; and what is its point of orgination, they are inflexible. These responses of value are based on the religious paradigm devoid of physical data regarding the process of pregnancy.

I am proposing a reversal of the above approach. The ethician must begin with the medical and biological facts and weigh them carefully in the light of (1) the religious memory of the moral tradition; (2) the operational validity of the moral principles; (3) and, if necessary, a shaping of the paradigms and the creation of new constructs to respond to the problem. A sound method is to evaluate the extent of permissable "ethical flexibility" between the extremes of public policy and reflective ethical thought. This particular religious, though not necessarily biblical or spiritual, orientation affords us a view of life's value intrinsic to man's decision-making process.

Peter Berger, a contemporary sociologist with religious knowledge, has astutely observed that

> whatever may be the "ultimate" merits of religious explanations of the universe at large, their empirical tendency has been to falsify man's consciousness of that part of the universe shaped by his own activity, namely the socio-cultural world. This falsification can also be described as mystification. The socio-cultural world, which is an edifice of human meanings, is overlaid with mysteries posited as nonhuman in their origins. All human productions are, at least potentially, comprehensible in human

terms. The veil of mystification thrown over them by religion prevents such comprehension.[51]

All too often this is true. However, the religious element is usually not at fault. Rather, the institutionalization of spiritual, mediational values has caused that veil of mystification to be powerfully used. Much of what religion as an ethical attitude holds to be ultimate regarding the nature of the world and of man in the world can be witnessed biologically.[52] For example, the uniqueness of each individual—which is also part of the paradigmatic creation story —is represented by the DNA molecule—a paradoxical principle of unity and multiple forms of novelty.[53] While, on the one hand, DNA is a strong case for the uniqueness of life supported by variations in the very genetic code which we share as informing our biological makeup, on the other hand, DNA is a set of blueprints which, if lost or removed, can be repeated many times.[54]

In the foregoing critique, I have assumed the following: (1) a literal approach to scripture is *not* the only source of the "religious," or, of the "ultimate";[55] (2) the ethical questions of "life" and "what it means to be a human being" are as ambiguous as deciphering what it means to be God or what it means to know "God's will"; (3) all areas concerned—biomedical, science, philosophical, and religious investigations—are related to the comprehension of the enhancement of life, whether by the behavioristic acceptance of techniques of survival or by a more thoroughgoing and meaningful interpretation of the life processes; (4) any ethical or moral question exists in the context of the paradoxical. Men are not existential islands of solitary communion. *Man's only moment of solitariness is decision-making.* Man is socially involved and held accountable for a way of being. Paradoxically, he seems to make free decisions regarding himself but really he is limited by the consequences of his decision-making. We term this limit "responsibility." This ethical paradox confounds the ethician as he relates to the question of abortion since he is sorely tempted to put away the usual considerations and to render a normative judgment without examining the pertinent data from the sciences and without investigating the methodological options made possible by the contemporary religious ethicians.

All so-called moral behavior is rooted in the economic, political, and legal web of man's sociality. No one response or one aspect of man's sociality covers all aspects of his existence. As this extends to diverse cultures, it also applies to intracultural dimensions. For example, the Supreme Court decision regarding abortion may render the conditions for the legality of abortions, but it has not necessarily rendered any help to the individual process of decision-making. The religious quest of man is concerned with "truth values" since man operates on so many levels and in so many dimensions. Abortion, as the case in point, offers viable options also, since it relates to multiple levels of meaning. However, all dimensions must operate within a reconstructed "accepted life." Jürgen Moltmann, a theologian of hope, describes the value of "accepted life" as a criterion for a new image of being human.

> Where life cannot be accepted, loved and experienced, we are no longer dealing with human life. If a child does not feel that he is accepted, he becomes ill. If a person does not accept himself, he loses his vigor. If a life can no longer be experienced, it is dead. . . . Experienced life is a life that contains contradiction and finds the strength to include contradictions in itself and to endure them.[56]

Ambiguity and contradiction can only be countered by the decision-making process which allows man to move with an achieved sense of awareness. "Accepted life" as a principle, albeit a descriptive principle, might be a real possibility. However, as a concept, "accepted life" can only be viewed in the circle of dependent relationships which form the complex of the issue itself. While each aspect is distinct, some almost intangible tie binds one to the other. One of the most useful paradigms one can cite comes from the Buddhist philosophy of life and death, a causation series of relationships blending emotional and psychological ties of environment and self.

Considering only the course of human purpose—if "accepted life" suggests either a teleology or a concern for the soul—is insufficient. The encyclical of Pope Paul VI, *Humanae Vitae (On the Regulation of Birth)*[57] may deal with the teleological place of man in the directional perspective of the universe based upon the creation paradigm, but that may be little help to the plight of the Appalachian woman, for example, who is ignorant of the biological processes when having sexual intercourse. She is not at all concerned with the directional course of the nature of things. Her intention couldn't possibly consider the obvious or subtle religious and biblical arguments. Yet, she would be very ripe for moral imperatives under the guise of the spiritual. The spiritual satisfaction is easily substituted for more immediate needs when other satisfactions are denied. The moral imperative is null and void when we argue from a reasoning which states: "I know the *product* man: I know the *nature* of man: therefore, I know the *origin* of man." There is quite a leap from the product to the cause and that is where the problem lies, in the nature of man himself, or better still, in the nature of the "immortal soul."

However, the opposite situation from that of the Appalachian woman is the high rate of abortion "procedures" which deny any teleological direction of the universe. Mass abortions are performed out of a social concern for the population, the mental and physical condition of the women, or out of total indifference. The presence of "soul" or any quality is not considered in the discussion of abortion procedure. This is the other end of the pendulum.[58]

Within the Roman Catholic tradition the presence, maintenance, and future life of the soul for the glory of God have been of paramount importance. Is soul a working construct? If so, for whom? Certain conceptions of the soul, its generation and/or creation and presence, have historically come down to us in various forms from theological positions pertaining to the development of the embryo and fetus. For example, Tertullian held that the soul came into existence as a biological transmission from Adam through one's immediate parents (*traducianism*). Clement of Alexandria held that the soul was directly created by God (*creationism*). Albert the Great held the principle of *simultaneous animation*. Augustine claimed that no soul was present until the moment of "quickening," i.e., the moment when the mother-to-be detected the first stirrings of life within her body. Against the prevailing ideas of the creationist view (and other views such as those of the Pelagians), Augustine claimed that the Bible does not offer conclusive proof of the direct creation of the soul by God or of the natural presence of the soul through the natural process of procreative activity. Thomas Aquinas, on the other hand, discusses the *infusion* of the soul at about the fortieth day in the male embryo and about the eightieth day in the female embryo after *successive animation*, i.e., the process of develoment from vegetable, animal, to human soul. Papal encyclicals from Pope Innocent IX (1679) and Pope Pius XI (1930) sacralize the inviolability of the fetal life. Pope Innocent contended that it is prohibited to hold any longer that "no homicide is committed in any abortion."[59] Later, distinctions were drawn between direct abortions and indirect abortions implying the principle of double effect, i.e., if an abortion is an indirect result of an operation to help the woman with another physical disorder, it is not homicide.

A contemporary Roman Catholic theologian, Bernard Häring, in his new book, *Medical Ethics*, takes a markedly liberal position compared with the church's teaching and with his earlier work, *The Law of Christ*.[60] Concerning the relationship among the authority of the Pope, the teaching authority of the church, and biomedical decision-making, Reverend Häring suggests:

> On questions of morality, the *rôle* of infallibility is limited to the enunciation of the most basic principles, to declaring, for instance, the fundamental right of man to life and prohibiting unjust killing. In moral matters not predicated by divine revelation but resulting from shared experience and co-reflection, the magisterium . . . cannot speak without giving its reasons and the pastoral meaning of its position.
>
> Since the magisterium speaks on the specific problems of a particular time and with the tools of a definite cultural period, the theologian must be a master of hermeneutics, that is, the art of exegesis in the light of the historical context, mindful always of the actual occasion on which the magisterium spoke and fully aware of the degree of certainty or probability. If the utterance of the magisterium is no longer in tune with new insights and the modern context, physicians and theologians have a joint obligation to look for better solutions and, if need be, to inform the magisterium of this. . . . The final court is the conscience of the physician and/or that of the patient, taking fully into ac-

count the doctrine of the magisterium and the endeavors of theologians and other ethicists without which a doctor could not arrive at a thoroughly well-informed decision of conscience.[61]

His conclusions regarding the origin of human life rest on: (1) the lack of knowledge regarding the precise moment of hominization; (2) individualism does not occur until the basic brain structure has fully developed; (3) the fetus is involved in a developing process even though we cannot predict exactly each step of the process.[62] "I think it can be said that at least before the twenty-fifth to fortieth day, the embryo cannot yet (with certainty) be considered as a human person; or, to put it differently, that about that time the embryo becomes a being with all the basic rights of a human person." For Reverend Häring, human life is defined as *"personal existence in a live body which is the substratum of the spiritual life principle."*[63]

Like his Protestant colleagues, Reverend Häring, in his honest approach to a very delicate issue within the church, is thinking and speaking more boldly than before. It is apparent that what was once an intimate connection between theologian and the church hierarchy is drifting into decision-making on the part of the individual theologian. It is very difficult to speak of an official position which all clergy and believers in Roman Catholic tradition will hold. And yet the official position claiming tradition is being spoken by such ecclesiastical authorities as Archbishop Krol at Senate subcommittee hearings and Bishop Leo T. Maher in his admonition to the NOW organization in San Diego for their pro-abortion stand. The progressive position of Reverend Häring's goes markedly away from the traditional and present anti-abortion, pro-life argument.

Abortion, in the Roman Catholic view, is defined as the taking of a human life. This definition has popularly been accepted and any act of termination of pregnancy has unfortunately been called "abortion." Abortion is never licit as a birth control method. It can be accepted only as an indirect effect of surgery to save the mother from some medical disorder other than pregnancy—whether the aborted one was healthy or diagnosed as genetically unhealthy, or brain damaged.[64] From this absolute position, other theologians have moved their arguments from the question of the soul to the question of the "potential for life" to the spiritual values which the problematic of abortion seems obviously to violate. The argument has moved away from "soul" although concern with immortality and soul are psychologically pressing. "Soul" and "immortality" operate in a mythological way. These constructs bind important values to the life process but they are limited to concern for the individual. "The myth of the soul expresses a faith in the intrinsic value of the human individual as an end in himself."[65] The opposite position, taken by Harmon Smith, defines soul as "the lasting value-in-relationship which we attach and attribute to human beings."[66]

Within the Protestant traditions, consensus is difficult to state simply. Besides the denominational statements, contemporary theologians freely explore and speak on biomedical issues. A survey of religious views on abortion was recently done by Arthur J. Dyck, of Harvard University. He worked as part of a team from the Institute of Society, Ethics, and the Life Sciences investigating population policy.[67] "Protestant views range from those that favor abortion when the life and health of the mother is seriously threatened to those who favor abortion on request."[68]

In addition to those statements cited by Professor Dyck is a very recent statement (1974) by the American Lutheran Church revising its position of 1966. In 1966 the church recognized therapeutic reasons for abortion. The Lutheran Church in America, in a policy statement of 1970, asserted that "the fetus is the organic beginning of human life," and "the determination of its development is always a serious matter." Responsible decisions regarding abortion are based on "the life and total health of the mother, her responsibility toward others in her family, the stage of development of the fetus, the economic and psychological stability of the home, the laws of the land, and the consequences to society as a whole.[69]

> A decision on abortion is too serious to be solely a personal decision. It is a decision which should be guided, but not forced, by church, by law, by public opinion, by family, and by other trusted persons. It is a decision toward which the Christian

community ought to offer its tender, embracing, and understanding love and help. Pastors, church councils, auxiliaries, and key persons in agencies and institutions related to the American Lutheran Church need to give leadership toward assuring that competent counseling services are available for persons considering an abortion.[70]

On the other hand, within Protestantism, theologians offer diverse rationale and pursue a theological perspective of their own construction, while they maintain a church affiliation. Paul Ramsey, a Methodist, and Helmut Thielicke, a German Lutheran, have also spoken in favor of the autonomous rights of the fetus. Paul Ramsey structures his response around the relationship of God and man as symbolized by the biblical covenant. Professor Ramsey states: "One grasps the religious outlook upon the sanctity of human life only if one sees that this life is asserted to be surrounded by sanctity that need not be in a man; that the most dignity a man ever possesses is a dignity that is alien to him. . . . A man's dignity arises from God's dealings with him, and not primarily in anticipation of anything he will ever have in him."[71] Helmut Thielicke is opposed to abortion on the principle of the possible parenthood represented by the becoming process of nascent life.[72] Both men are concerned with the question of the morality or immorality of the act itself. While they are interested in the surrounding issues, their major concern is the issue of the fetus.

The most controversial position regarding abortion is taken by Joseph Fletcher, a liberal Protestant and a pioneer in the area of medical ethics, with the publication of *Morals and Medicine* in 1954. The ambiguity of his situational morality rests in his claim that the personality is the indicator of a human being. Professor Fletcher rejects fertilization or any other fixed biological and/or physical point as definitive of whatever it means to be human and personal.[73] In a recent article for the *Hastings Center Report,* Professor Fletcher outlines a profile of what is man.

> Synthetic concepts such as *human* and *person* require operational terms, spelling out the which and what and when. Only in that way can we get down to cases—to normative decisions.

There are always some people who prefer to be visceral and affective in their moral choices, with no desire to have any rationale for what they do. But ethics is precisely the business of rational, critical reflection (encephalic and not merely visceral) about the problems of the moral agent. . . .

To that end, then, for the purposes of biomedical ethics, I am suggesting a "profile of man" in concrete and discrete terms.[74]

The profile he outlines consists of what he calls positive human criteria: minimal intelligence (signified by the rationale of above an I.Q. of 20), self-awareness, self-control, sense of time, a sense of the past, the capability to relate to others, concern for others, communication, control of existence, curiosity, change and changeability, balance of rationality and feeling, idiosyncrasy, and neocortical function. The last indicator is the most important. "Personal reality depends on cerebration and to be dead 'humanly' speaking is to be ex-cerebral, no matter how long the body remains alive."[75]

The negative human criteria are also outlined. (1) "Man is non- or anti-artificial." The problem here is to define artificiality. Fletcher claims that an accepted test-tube baby would be less artificial than an unwanted baby resulting from "sexual roulette." (2) "Man is not essentially parental." (3) "Man is not essentially sexual." (4) "Man is not a bundle of rights." Man is not simply a nature, composed of a priori ideas such as "a sense of oughtness," "original sin" as if they were objective, preexistent ideas. (5) "Man is not a worshipper." "Faith in supernatural realities and attempts to be in direct association with them are choices some human beings make and others do not. Mystique is not essential to being truly a person."[76]

The liberal and humanistic side of me wants to give a positive vote for the common-sense of this position. The more conservative side wants something more. I am not content with an operational perspective which cannot deal with the origin of human life itself—the physical act of the process of organic development. Can an operational approach touch the biological process with as much assurance as Profsesor Fletcher has touched the perceptual and phenomenological aspects of the question of abortion and related matters? I believe that some attempts have been made in the area of an operational approach to the process of the origin of human life and we must work with perceptions of this data rather than peripheral concerns.

Before proceeding to a discussion of what I have interpreted as operational attempts, I would like to state briefly the traditional Jewish approaches to sexuality and woman. Since Judaica offers a distinct paradoxical emphasis on both a concern for the woman and the *mitzvah* of procreation. Jewish theology also offers polar views of the status of the fetus. The contemporary literature on the question is scarce. In the Jewish attitude toward sexuality, based upon the religious duty of marriage, the question of children is but one aspect, albeit an important one, of the relationship. However, marital relations are seen as the duty of the husband and the privilege of the wife. Sexual pleasure and the woman's well-being are co-important with procreation.[77] When, and for what reasons, contraceptives are to be used are clearly spelled out. Yet, in the present abortion controversy we are confronted with extreme positions:

> Feldman (1968) identifies what is the consensus of Jewish law: That therapeutic abortion up to the moment of birth is mandated by the *Mishnah* to save the woman's life, to save her life even to the point of the emergence of the fetus when death to both is the alternative. If one asks about cases that fall outside the consensus, Feldman identifies two distinct schools of thought in Jewish law. One school assumes no real prohibition against abortion except, perhaps, in the most advanced stages of pregnancy, and then proceeds to build up safeguards against indiscriminate abortion. The second school sees abortion as akin to homicide, permissible for saving the life of a pregnant woman and then, in its consideration of various cases, embraces grave threats to health as a justification for abortion.[78]

A particularly vocal interpretation of Jewish law, however, is that the fetus has the inalienable right to life except in grave cases where the life of the mother, not the condition of the fetus, is gravely threatened.[79] Statements issued by the General Assembly of the American Hebrew Congregation (1967) urged humane legislation in abortion reform. On the other hand, Rabbi Meyer

Cohen, executive director of the Union of Orthodox Rabbis of the United States and Canada (1971), stressed the prohibition of abortion in Jewish law as well as a rejection of legislation on the subject. The sanctity of life is undermined and the innocent and defenseless life of an unborn child is at stake.[80]

At the recent Senate subcommittee hearings, opposing views were presented. Balfour Brickner, a rabbi and national director of the Commission on Interfaith Activities, represented the Union of American Hebrew Congregations. He suggested that the fetus in the womb was not a person until it was born. He also added that most of the objections to abortion, as rightly observed by the American Law Institute, were based on religious beliefs which deemed abortion as sinful.[81] Rabbi David Bleich upheld protection for fetal life under the same safeguards as other members.[82]

In all of the religious traditions, whether as institutions or represented by theologians and ministers interpreting tradition, we are still left with the problem of dealing with the taboo question of the origin of life. The positions in most instances are polarized. Either the life of the mother—for physical, psychological, or sociological reasons—is the cause for the permission for abortion, or the act of abortion is deemed sinful because of the innocence of fetal life. In no instance is the process of fetal development seen to be made up of instants of differing structures and activities so as to produce distinct positions for distinct trimesters of activity. At least the Supreme Court decision was able to render a decision on the basis of observations relating to periods of development. Yet, theologians, who are grounded in the paradigm of the creation event as repeated through the act of reproduction in the process of life, see one activity. Many are unable to glimpse discrete moments in which change takes place and makes something other than it was. By categorizing the act of abortion as "murder," we are standing in a judgment which has a history of speculative reasoning about the nature of man behind it. A more rigid interpretation of biblical and certain theological traditions confines us to a moralistic judgment which refuses to listen to other possible meanings of the "Judeo-Christian story" with its intentional and paradigmatic value.[83] Moralistic judgments do not benefit the ignorant, nor enlighten the learned. They merely stop the progress of the consciousness of man by closing the possibility of novelty and growth through novelty. Charles Hartshorne has said it most aptly in his understanding of the paradoxical nature of the issue:

> Obviously there is a case against abortion. It is a violent interference with a natural process which in essence is beneficent. But I have for years combated the idea that abortion is wrong simply because it is murder. The proper meaning of the last word is, the killing of a human person by a human person. Now an embryo is not a person, but the possibility or the probability of there being a person many months or even years in the future. A person is a conscious individual, able to think, at least as a speaking animal can think, or—if God is personal—able to think on a still higher level than that which depends upon language. An ape may be closer to thinking in the human sense than an embryo is. Exclusively, with respect to other remote future possibilities, not with respect to actualities, has an embryo any thinking capacity. Obviously, possibilities are important, but to blur the distinction between them (possibilities) and actualities is to darken counsel. So I say an embryo is not a person, and abortion is not murder.[84]

A discussion of the ontological status of the fetus in process to which I will refer is found in "The Ontology of Abortion." Professor H. Tristam Engelhardt defines the ontological status in this way:

> By this is meant the quandry of determining whether or to what extent the fetus is a person. Thus, by the ontological status I shall mean certain general categories of being, such as being an inanimate object, being a mere animal, being a fully developed self-conscious human person. With regard to the question of abortion, this is the issue of whether the fetus shows itself to be something to which one owes obligations in the sense one owes obligations to persons.[85]

The question has two poles of understanding: ontological and operational.

> The ontological issue is the meaning of "human person" vis-à-vis "human life"—the issue of distinguishing the significance of two

categories: one ethical, the other biological. The operational question arises in deciding what measurable criteria justify the statement that a person now exists where none existed previously. In this question, more is involved than a clarification of the categories of reality. Analogously to the proof of the existence of the immortal soul in medieval philosophy, here a proof or disproof of the presence or absence of at least a mortal human soul is required for the identification of the existence of psychological (or personal), not merely biological, "reality."[86]

First, Professor Engelhardt stresses the metaphorical character of the language "he/she" uses to describe the fetus *in utero.* "The metaphorical character of such speech suggests that its object does not fall within the usual limits of personal life, that there may be merely human life present but not a person."[87] He is attempting to describe the limits of personal life vis-à-vis human life, and not to give, as Joseph Fletcher has done, a profile of personal life.

Professor Engelhardt considers the decision of the Ad Hoc Committee of the Harvard Medical School to Examine the Definition of Brain Death and the Ad Hoc Committee of the American Electroencephalographic Society on EEG Criteria for Determination of Cerebral Death.

[They] have argued that: 1) the brain is the physical substratum of conscious life and 2) one can consequently decide when death occurs by *appropriate operational parameters* [my emphasis] which indicate the destruction of the brain as an intact functioning organ. It was decided that a prolonged flat electroencephalograph (in the absence of particular distorting conditions) is a true index of the destruction of the higher central nervous system and, thus, indicates that death has occurred. Importantly, the crucial level of life is more than the mere continuance of biological life. Biological life, in the sense of the integrated function of all other organs and the lower elements of the central nervous system, continues even in the presence of brain death.[88]

Personal life has ended with brain death. The question is: Can the same criterion, i.e., an active EEG, be the same operational principle for the determination of personal life as distinct from human life? Indeed the ontological status of a human being is changed if death is declared according to the criteria established by the Harvard Commission Study. Distinctions are made between two orders of human being. The question is now asked, is there substantial continuity from conception to death?[89]

The argument in the affirmative begins with the principle that there is one substance present through the history of the being involved. Rationality is in potency in every embryo. Thus, the fetus is what it will be. The argument erroneously proceeds from effect to cause. To this Professor Engelhardt replies: "The value of a potential future state endows an object with value, but not the actual value of the future state. To account for continuity and future value through a metaphysical doctrine of potentiality or substance (i.e., one in which the potential has real status and defines the "substance" of an object *ab initio*) involves serious difficulties."[90] The recommendation which he makes involves a developmental approach from biological life to personal properties with a consequent essential and substantial change in the being under discussion.[91] This position is most significant. Emphasizing indirectly an attitude of process within a constructive sense of operationalism he points in a direction not yet heard in biomedical ethics. He does point out that, while Thomas Aquinas' principle of the development of human ontogeny does service to the developmental process, it is still insufficient to account for qualitative personal life on the basis of quantitative change. Mediate animation, that is, the presence of the soul at various stages of human ontogeny, bears the suggestion of a processive change, but in actuality it does not begin with that premise. Thomas Aquinas begins with the premise that there are different kinds of souls, vegetable, animal, and human rational which occur consequently to each other thus recapitulating the levels of creation within the progression. Once again, the accountability for different levels of human significance, as well as utilizing this accountability to rsepond to the question of abortion, has not sufficiently been done.

"Human life is an unbroken continuum which not only extends from one person to another but to the very origin of terrestrial life."[92] Within this continuum there exist quantitative and qualitative changes. The problem of determining what relationship occurs with what value is the difficulty. "In the case of a human being, one has a continuum beginning with the formation of the zygote at conception, progressing to the development of a rational human being, and ending after cerebral death in mere biological existence. When focusing on the continuum between the zygote and the mature person, the ends of the spectrum appear qualitatively distinct, though no particular quantitative change identified a development of a status different in kind."[93] Various operational concepts have been and are presently being used to define the legal and personal aspects of the fetus: (1) ensoulment, (2) quickening or movement inside the womb (human movements), (3) viability, or the ability of the fetus to live outside the womb and as such to bear a social status, (4) child. Professor Engelhardt suggests relational qualities toward the acceptance of viability, as distinct from the simple biological definition to determine a human being. Other socially defined contexts will enable the fetus to be defined as an independent though not yet personal entity. In the social context of a relational world view actual obligations persist toward the viable fetus. In the interest of protecting against infanticide, this difference of viability is important. In the latter concern, other norms such as communication patterns and competition alter the ethical questions.

This article raises the question of the distinction between human biological life and personal life by appealing to the ontological and operational status of the being under discussion. Applying the ontological description of the status of the human being at death, identifiable with the flat EEG, is to locate that which is personal in the adequate functioning of the brain and the nervous system. Using this same perspective with regard to the fetus does not work in quite the same way, or at least we do not feel as comfortable about it. The criteria of ensoulment that derive from Aristole's and, consequently, Aquinas' levels of substantial existence, while healthy in the processive approach, base their distinctions on rather arbitrary and medically ignorant concepts. Quickening indicates a different phase, but not necessarily a different qualitative change in the status of the fetus, while viability does offer a social relationship now possible because the umbilical cord may be severed, establishing child as a social category. (This precludes any argument which bases its rationale on the relationship between mother and child.)

In "The Ethical Problems of Abortion," Sissela Bok offers some additional insights into the different ontological perspectives offered above (although she does not use the term "ontological").[94] Within the basic conflict "between a pregnant woman and the unborn life she harbors," Professor Bok determines areas of ethical responsibility for the mother and for society. First, abortion may be thought of as withdrawal of bodily support on the part of the mother.[95] In agreeing with Judith Thompson "that the mother who finds herself pregnant as a result of a rape or in spite of every precaution, does not have the obligation to continue the pregnancy." Professor Bok affirms that cessation of continued support suggests that the woman determines the right to use another person's body. I would add that the relational factor is most important here. The decision is based on the presence or absence of a positive relationship to that which is borne. Within the context of the cessation of bodily support, i.e., viability, the ontological status of the fetus changes once again because of the social-legal definition established by public policy.

The larger question which concerns Professor Bok is "whether the life of the fetus should receive the same protection as other lives—whether killing the fetus, by whatever means, and for whatever reasons, is to be thought of as killing a human being."[96] Beginning with John Noonan's Catholic position that if you are conceived by human parents you are human, she distinguishes varying stages of the developmental process—implantation, conception, embryonic stage (two to four weeks after conception), looking human (six weeks), the development of the brain (eight weeks), quickening, viability, and the process of birth itself. She does not maintain that the presence of brain waves is indicative of the presence of a human life. "For the lack of brain response at the end of life has to be shown to be irreversible in order to support a conclusion that life is absent. The lack of response from the embryo's brain, on the other hand, is temporary and precisely not irreversible."[97] But the problem, she claims, lies

113

not in the factual information which we possess. The views which accept one or another of the above criteria seek to conceptualize the process by the terms "humanity," "human life," "human individual," "person," etc.

> [They] are representative of different world views, often of a religious nature, involving deeply held commitments with moral consequences. There is no disagreement as to what we know about life and its development before and after conception; differences arise only about the names and moral consequences we attach to the changes in this development and the distinctions we consider important. . . . Our efforts to pinpoint and to define, reflect the urgency with which we reach for abstract labels and absolute certainty in facts and in nature; . . .[98]

While abandoning the search for a definition of humanity, she searches for the reasoning for holding life sacred (1) by discussing the rationale for protecting life by appealing to why killing is disdained, (2) by applying the parádox to the relational characteristics immanent in the fetal stages of development. Basically, killing causes suffering, anguish, the loss of the value of life for the victim. Obviously, then, on the basis of this rationale, killing an embryo is not killing at all. On the other hand, infanticide would violate the principle of the preservation of life by causing the above harmful effects. Within the continuum of pregnancy, lines can be drawn between the first part and the second part of later pregnancy. She emphasizes quickening and viability as indicators of limitation to the decision-making process rather than determinants of humanity. Society has a stake in the viable fetus. Morality and the case of the right thing to do has the advantage in the case of quickening, except when the life of the mother is in danger. Professor Bok orders moral distinctions based on conditions, such as the intentionality of the woman, the reasons for wanting the abortion, the time of the pregnancy, and religious views. Further, she acknowledges the paradoxical intention of abortion laws over against the individual's purposes and limitations.

I have highlighted the importance of these two articles because they reflect a wrestling with the most important issue in the question of abortion and that is whether or not a justifiable moral "construct"—abortion—is warranted in all cases of terminating a pregnancy. This is based on the view that pregnancy is a developmental process; each stage is different from the one before; each stage is subject to its own options in the decision-making process for both the individual and society. We have also seen that the quest for personal existence in terms of neo-cortical and brain activity creates differences of opinion when applied to the fetus, while the quest for a definition of humanity is a paradoxical one. The way is open for a continued expression of the ethical distinctions in the process itself.

Returning to the Buddhist perspective, I believe that the process of abstraction entailed in the description of the coming-to-be, which is the never-ending process of life itself, allows choice within a fluid world. The developmental approach which Professors Bok and Engelhardt have outlined, while extremely valuable, will inevitably be lost because the assumption which grounds them is not so fluid as the ethical distinctions they offer. For example, within the Western idea of biological life and personal life, the search is for the personal, as if it were a thing to be limited and easily defined. Professor Hartshorne expresses it in this way:

> Personal identity is an abstraction; concretely, each of us is a new reality every moment. The Buddhists saw this long ago and realized intuitively, through meditation and cultivation of altruistic sentiments that "self" and "other" are simplifications that miss much of the real structure of life. Their "no soul, no substance" doctrine was a result of this insight. *I now* am not simply "identical" with *me yesterday* or *me tomorrow*. A subject is not identical with its own object, and I now have myself as past or future only as object. The present I is the subject for which my past or future selves are objects. And my friend or enemy is also my object. There is, or may be, a degree of identification with all of these objects, but since none of them is more than temporary, therefore, thought, which makes all the future its object, cannot be satisfied with any of them as absolute values. The real goal and criterion of value must be something beyond the spatial and temporal limitations of localized animal life altogether.[99]

Personal identity then is the ignorance of which the Buddhist speaks as the first precondition. Within the twelve-linked Chain of Causation this ignorance is responsible for *karma* or the conformations of thought, impressions, the effects of work, and merit of action. All cause life in the present. This does not mean that there is a deliberate will causing action. A cosmic causality works also to balance the individual process. Consciousness works at many levels. Consciousness is interpreted as a "primitive mental operation taking place at the very time when a living being enters the maternal womb."[100] The combination of ignorance and conformations could indeed describe the congenital factors—hereditary characteristics, positive and negative—within the explosion of prenatal trauma. Within such an operational perspective, the building of constructs will function to create meaning across multi-dimensional relationships. Such constructs must be based on the data revealed in the process of fetal development. They must also reflect the imaginative use of the processive world view which grounds the operational aspect of fetal ontology.

Religious ethics must come to grips with the concrete issue of abortion at the point of the origin of life itself. Whether we use the construct "human" or "personal" depends upon the perspective in which we ground the epistemological parameters of our issue. If we choose a process philosophical approach, then ontology will be revealed in the impermanence of the relationship established between the poles of existence—self and other, or individual and society. I contend that the only point of certainty within a process approach is in the decision to do something. Whether one chooses to have or not to have an abortion, the issue revolves about the process of deciding itself.

I have further contended that the decision may be based on a more viable option than traditional spiritual values have rendered. In an organic view of the human body one is left with the inseparable unity of diverse functions which complement the harmony of the cosmic process itself. Within the actual entities which each stage of the fetal process represents, we have imagined a Buddhist conceptualization as an illustration of the process from birth to death. This paradigm and the attending construct of the twelve preconditions may operate in relation with the biological data in a more precise effort to suggest options for decision-making. While I agree with both Professors Engelhardt and Bok on the ethical distinctions they draw, I wonder if the distinctions will be cogent from the religious realm which grounds the stages themselves? I have suggested that a process world view is indispensable to the possibility of appropriate constructs to deal with the abortion issue. Just as the moral taboos have come from the realm of the spiritual, the revised ethical positions must come from the realm of the religious. Man cannot expect to approach this task without reevaluating the traditions and their paradigms which have established the taboos in the first place.

Within the Judeo-Christian story, there are few paradigms which can be reshaped without simply doing what theologians have been doing in the name of demythologization. Process theologians are trying to maintain the paradigms of the Judeo-Christian story while at the same time suggesting what I have termed "constructs" for operational theology. However, the plight of the theologian is an institutional and traditional heritage which establishes a priori the limits of spirituality. It is this element, spirituality, which is usually placed in the sphere of the pragmatic reality of decision-making. Spirituality is inoperable in this sphere. I do not believe that a necessarily consistent position between the two is possible. The decision-making process must be put within a neutral framework of an abstracted ontology and epistemology which may or may not be compatible with Christianity *per se* or with Judaism *per se*. Within the traditions models differ from one another considerably. For example, the Reform Jewish appreciation of Torah and the Orthodox appreciation of Torah are significantly different to create different modes of behavior and consequently different values. The sharp differences among denominations on the abortion issue cause one to ask the model of Christianity and of Christ which forms the basis of each position offered. The spiritual function of the traditions of Christianity and Judaism can inform the memory of man and so reshape the paradigms in the light of man's present context but it can only inform to the point of establishing reverence for values, respect for relationships and exemplary mediators of truths. These can only be verified in the decision to do so.

I am not going to conclude by reshaping the paradigms. I am simply going to say that the paradigms will be reshaped each time a decision is made in the epistemological parameters of religious ethics. What John Cobb has called "ontological realism"[101] is more than an awareness that Christian theology is possible; it is awareness that the separate religious traditions of the past have joined together in the present of man's history in a critical, ethical, ontological realism. A Whiteheadian religious approach is precisely "what one does with his solitariness."[102] However, I applaud, for example, the effort of David Griffin, a process theologian, to give a direction to Christian existence in a process Christology.[103] The options for the creation of constructs are no longer limited to the paradigms of one tradition. For the scientific study of religion has revealed that the quest for the truth of man is a common universe of discourse not limited by time, space, or one model. To build a common universe of discourse demands (1) an ontological framework, (2) a processive view of man and nature, (3) epistemological parameters, (4) a process of decision-making. This is a philosophy of religion which operates in the actual concretization of thought in activity. It is an extrapolation of Alfred North Whitehead's process philosophy toward a process ethics.

The emerging ethician may employ an operational process ethic in his "risk-taking opportunity" which is being presented to him in bioethics. In his search for meaningful constructs by which to suggest options for the decision-making process he confronts the paradox of the individual and the social. It is only in this confrontation that the personal is born. Contrary to Professor Engelhardt's position, the personal is not a category to be sought in one activity of the fetal process. The personal is established only by the relationship quality borne out of a mutual acceptance by the individuals of which a society is made. The ethician suggests ground rules, options, and processes. He draws upon the operational constructs of various disciplines and tests them in the realm of normative thought and behavior. He examines the process into which, as well as out of which, constructs come. Maintaining an integrity for the past, he relates to the present in the hope that the future will inherit a worthwhile wisdom. The task of the ethician is religious in the most crucial sense. But it is not spiritual.

When the ethician relates to the fetal process, he is relating to a concrete issue involving the question of the origin of life. The sacral quality of this effort need not be located in spiritual imperatives, moral or otherwise. The sacral quality is inherent within the issue as the facts reveal. The process itself is valuable. The emphasis, then, is on the way one relates to the process. I have dismissed from consideration the extremist positions, traditionally religious and otherwise, which regard the fetus as inviable or the environmental conditions of the mother and society as being one-dimensional. The importance of these factors resides in the process of life and death to which they relate. Intensity of feeling and interest have given them a prominent place in bioethical discussion of abortion but that is putting the cart before the horse. Understanding the process itself is the cause for our concern. Premature perfection, either in the form of premature conclusions regarding the nature of life and death, or in the form of liberal considerations in favor of sociological and psychological considerations, do an injustice to the evolution of man and the unfolding of his history.

The emerging ethician becomes precise only by ascertaining the paradox which he is asked to confront. Technique is operable only under the honest appraisal of what it is we are manipulating. Within religious thought we have imagined concepts of God, man, the universe in the paradigms of creation, the fall of man, the covenant, and the promise. Our Eastern religious thinkers have undertaken the very same task without the benefit of technique in the postindustrial sense of the word. Yet, as Buddhism has illustrated, they have attempted to imagine the stages of growth—preconditions for what is—with similar reverence for the holy, the self, and the cosmos. Eastern paradigms include the cyclical pattern of human and cosmic history, the presence of an absolute—in the case of Buddhism, a nonabsolute absolute—and a reverence for the ecological spirit which creates its own *karma*. What makes the difference among paradigms? Simply *the decision* to act out one form

119

of imagination over against another. If we dismiss the difference as cultural relativism, we throw the freedom and responsibility of creative selfhood to the reality around us. This is technological precision at its worst because it takes from man the wisdom which his memory and decision-making process have relegated to his care. Choosing models of reality out of which to operate is the task of the individual. Pointing out those models is the task of the emerging ethician.

NOTES

1. Van Rensselaer Potter, *Bioethics: Bridge to the Future* (Englewood Cliffs, N.J.: Prentice-Hall, 1971), pp. 1–2.

2. "Science indeed cannot create, derive or propose values. But the pursuit of objective knowledge is in itself an ethical attitude, founded upon an internal *choice* of a value system, which I shall call 'the ethics of knowledge.'" Jacques Monod, "On the Logical Relationship between Knowledge and Values," in *The Biological Revolution: Social Good or Social Evil*, ed. Watson Fuller (Garden City, N.Y.: Doubleday [Anchor], 1972), p. 16.

3. Daniel Callahan, "Bioethics as a Discipline," *Hastings Center Studies* I, no. 1, 1973, p. 71.

4. Ibid., pp. 72–73.

5. Ibid., p. 72.

6. Ibid., p. 73.

7. Paul Ramsey, "The Nature of Medical Ethics," in *The Teaching of Medical Ethics,* ed. Veatch, Gaylin, and Morgan (Hastings-on-Hudson, N.Y.: Hastings Center, 1973), p. 18.

8. Ibid., pp. 18–19. See note 14.

9. Ibid., p. 19.

10. Ibid., p. 20.

11. Professor Ramsey cites John Rawls, *A Theory of Justice* (Cambridge, Mass.: Belknap Press of Harvard University Press, 1971). I suggest the reshaping (my term) of the principle of distributive justice.

12. Leon R. Kass, "The New Biology: What Price Relieving Man's Estate?" *Science* CLXXIV (November 19, 1971), p. 781.

13. Ibid., p. 782.

14. Robert M. Veatch, "Does Ethics Have an Empirical Basis?" *Hastings Center Studies* I, no. 1, 1973, p. 64.

15. Ibid.

16. Ibid.

17. Charles Hartshorne, "Beyond Enlightened Self-Interest: A Metaphysics of Ethics," *Ethics* LXXXIV, no. 3 (April 1974), p. 211.

18. Senator Walter F. Mondale in his statement on *The Proposal for the Establishment of the National Commission on Health, Science, and Society,* Joint Resolution 145, found in the National Commission on Health, Science, and Society Hearings before the Subcommittee on Government Research of the Committee on Government Operations, U.S. Senate, 90th Congress, March 7, 1968, p. 6.

19. Institute of Society, Ethics, and the Life Sciences, The Hastings Center, 623 Warburton Avenue, Hastings-on-Hudson, N.Y., 10706.

20. *H.R. 7724* in the Senate of the United States, March 21, 1974: *An Act to Amend the Public Health Service Act.*

21. Ibid., sec. 1201 and sec. 1202. Previously Joint Resolution 75 had established a National Advisory Commission on Health, Science, and Society to provide for a study and evaluation of the ethical, social, and legal implications of advances in biomedical research and technology.

22. Joshua Lederberg in his statement regarding Senate Joint Resolution 145, March 7, 1968, p. 55; cf. pp. 282–288.

23. Kenneth Vaux in his statement regarding Senate Joint Resolution 145, March 21, 1968, p. 137.

24. Robert L. Shinn, "Perilous Progress in Genetics," *Social Research* IV, no. 1 (Spring 1974), p. 83.

25. Cf. James M. Gustafson, "Basic Ethical Issues in the Biomedical Fields," *Soundings* LIII, no. 2 (Summer 1970), pp. 151–180. Cf. Eugene Fontinell, "Toward an Ethics of Relationship," in *Situationism and the New Morality,* ed. R. L. Cunningham (New York: Appleton-Century-Crofts, 1970). Professor Fontinell does insist that the most important aspect of these terms is how we understand them. He later states, ". . . every ethic depends implicitly or explicitly upon the way in which man views himself and his world, upon some kind of metaphysical perspective or world view. An effort to achieve a greater consciousness of ourselves and the world is a first step in any ethic," pp. 204–205.

26. Cf. Michael Polanyi, *Personal Knowledge: Towards a Post-Critical Philosophy* (New York and Evanston: Harper & Row [Harper Torchbooks], 1964).

27. Charles Hartshorne, "Ethics and the Process of Living," a lecture delivered at the conference on "Religion, Ethics and the Life Process" at the Institute of Religion and Human Development, Texas Medical Center, Houston, Texas, March 18–19, 1974.

28. Edward Conze, *Buddhism: Its Essence and Development,* with a preface by Arthur Waley (New York: Harper & Row [Harper Torchbooks], 1951, reprinted by arrangement with Bruno-Cassirer, Ltd., Oxford, 1951), pp. 130–131.

29. Ibid., p. 134.

30. Sögen Yamakami, *Systems of Buddhistic Thought* (Calcutta: University of Calcutta, 1912), pp. 8–9.

31. Ananda K. Coomaraswamy, *Buddha and the Gospel of Buddism* (New York: Harper & Row [Harper Torchbooks], 1964), p. 355.

32. William K. Frankena, *Ethics* (Englewood Cliffs, N.J.: Prentice-Hall,

1963), p. 14: as quoted by Daniel Callahan, "Ethics and Population Control," An Occasional Paper of the Population Council, 1971, p. 11.

33. Richard H. Robinson, *The Buddhist Religion: A Historical Introduction* (Belmont, Calif.: Dickenson, 1970), pp. 21–22.

34. Cf. Alfred E. Emerson and Ralph Wendell Burhoe, "Evolutionary Aspects of Freedom, Death and Dignity," *Zygon* IX, no. 2 (June 1974), pp. 156–182.

35. Ibid., p. 166.

36. Ibid.

37. Cf. Rogert Wertheimer, "Understanding the Abortion Argument," *The Rights and Wrongs of Abortion*, a Philosophy and Public Affairs Reader (Princeton: Princeton University Perss, 1973), pp. 68–69. Mr. Wertheimer denies the worthwhileness of a discussion of the "value of fetal life in its various stages." Instead he asks: "When does a human life begin?" Cf. notes 38 and 39 below. To my way of thinking that answer cannot be known. What can be known is a description of what evolves in the fetal process. This informs decision-making in an ontological framework.

38. S. Chandrasekhar, *Abortion in a Crowded World: The Problem with Special Reference to India* (Seattle: University of Washington Press, 1974), p. 31.

39. Malcolm Potts, "The Problem of Abortion," in *Biology and Ethics*, ed. E. J. Ebling (London and New York: Academic Press, 1969), pp. 74–75, as quoted in Chandrasekhar, *Abortion*, p. 31.

40. "The Beginning of Life," *Time* CIII, no. 25 (June 24, 1974), pp. 78–80.

41. Ibid., p. 79.

42. Peter Facione, "The Abortion Non-debate," *Cross Currents* (Fall 1973), book review, pp. 351–353. Cf. *A Review of Abortion and Social Justice* (New York: Sheed and Ward, 1968).

43. Ibid., p. 351.

44. Ibid., p. 353.

45. 93 S. Ct. 705 (1973); cf. *Congressional Quarterly Weekly Report*, March 16, 1974, p. 681.

46. 93 S. Ct. 739 (1973); cf. *Congressional Quarterly Weekly Report*, March 16, 1974, p. 681.

47. As stated in Emily C. Moore, "Abortion: The New Ruling," *Hastings Center Report* III, no. 4 (September 1973), p. 4.

48. *Congressional Quarterly Weekly Report*, March 16, 1974, p. 681; cf. *Genetic Counseling Newsletter* I, no. 1 (May 1973).

49. Ibid., p. 682.

50. Ibid. (Cf. Abortion Issues Background, 1973 *Weekly Report*, p. 2973); cf. John Bennett, "Avoid Oppressive Laws," *Christianity and Crisis* XXXII, no. 25 (January 8, 1973), p. 287. Congressman Father Robert Drinan advocates the repeal of laws governing abortion. Abortion should be in the hands of the medical profession and under the churches. He does not feel that the states should be burdened with the question.

51. Peter Berger, *The Sacred Canopy* (New York: Doubleday [Anchor Books], 1969 [1967]), p. 90.

52. Cf. R. W. Sperry, "Science and the Problem of Values," *Zygon* IX, no. 1, pp. 7–21.

53. For an excellent summary of the work of the DNA and RNA molecules, see "Man into Superman: The Promise and Peril of the New Genetics," *Time* XCVII, no. 16 (April 19, 1971), pp. 33–34.

54. Cf. Garrett Hardin, "Blueprints, DNA, and Abortion: A Scientific and Ethical Analysis," *Medical Opinion and Review* (February 1967), cited in Chandrasekhar, *Abortion*, pp. 29–31.

55. Paul Tillich defines "the ultimate" as "the unconditioned" (analogous to the Kantian notion of duty), but Tillich grounds "the ultimate" *as* and *in* being itself. Cf. *Systematic Theology*, vol. I (Chicago: University of Chicago Press, 1963).

56. Jürgen Moltmann, "Hope and the Biomedical Future of Man," in *Hope and the Future of Man*, ed. Ewert H. Cousins (Philadelphia: Fortress Press, 1972), p. 103. Originally a paper delivered at the Conference on Hope, Riverside Church, New York, N.Y. (October 1971). Cf. Judith Jarvis Thomson, "A Defense of Abortion," *Philosophy and Public Affairs* I (Fall 1971), p. 65.

57. Pope Paul VI, *Humanae Vitae. (On the Regulation of Birth)* (Montreal: Fides Publishing Co., 1968).

> Marriage is not, then, the effect of chance or the product of evaluation of unconscious natural forces; it is the wise institution of the Creator to realize in mankind His design of love. By means of reciprocal gift of self, proper and exclusive to them, husband and wife tend towards the communion of their beings in view of mutual personal perfection, to collaborate with God in the generation and education of new lives. [p. 7]

58. Cf. Daniel Callahan, "Abortion: Thinking and Experiencing," *Christianity and Crisis* XXXII, no. 23 (January 8, 1973), pp. 295–298.

59. Pope Innocent XI, *Errores doctrinae moralix laxioris*, 1679. See Harmon Smith, *Ethics and the New Medicine* (Nashville: Abingdon Press, 1970), no. 11, p. 29.

60. Bernard Häring, *Medical Ethics* (Notre Dame, Ind.: Fides, 1973); *The Law of Christ* (Westminster, Md.: Newman Press, 1961–1966).

61. Ibid., p. 37.

62. Ibid., p. 101.

63. Ibid., p. 84.

64. Cf. Pope Pius XII, Address to Large Families, 1951; cf. Pope Paul VI, *Humanae Vitae* (Boston: Daughters of St. Paul, 1968); cf. Arthur J. Dyck, *Religious Views and United States Population Policy*, Documentary Study Prepared for the Population Task Force of the Institute of Society, Ethics, and the Life Sciences as part of its study for the Commission on Population Growth and the American Future, 1971, pp. J-62–63.

65. John Hick, *Biology and the Soul* (Cambridge: Cambridge University Press, 1972), the 25th Arthur Stanley Eddington Memorial Lecture delivered at Cambridge University, February 1, 1972, p. 23.

66. Harmon L. Smith, *Ethics and the New Medicine*, p. 40.

67. Dyck, *Religious Views*.

68. Ibid., pp. 47–48.

69. Dyck, Religious Views, p. J-56; cf. Lutheran Church in America, *Sex, Marriage, and Family Social Statements* (New York: Board of Social Ministry, 1970), p. 5.

70. "Abortion and Christian Counsel," draft of a proposed statement and conviction approved by the executive committee of the Commission on Church and Society at its meeting on January 28, 1974, and recommended for adoption by the 1974 General Convention of the American Lutheran Church.

71. Paul Ramsey, "The Sanctity of Life," *The Dublin Review* 9241 (1967), pp. 3–23; cf. "The Morality of Abortion," in *Life or Death: Ethics and Options,* ed. Shils, et al., introduction by Daniel H. Labby (Portland, Ore.: Reed College, 1968), pp. 60–93: Both are cited by Smith, *Ethics and the New Medicine*; and Dyck, *Religious Views,* pp. J-52–J-55, p. 41.

72. Helmut Thielicke, *The Ethics of Sex,* trans. John W. Doberstein (New York: Harper & Row, 1964), pp. 226–247.

73. Cf. Smith, *Ethics and the New Medicine,* p. 40.

74. Joseph Fletcher, "Indicators of Humanhood: A Tentative Profile of Man," *Hastings Center Report* II, no. 5 (November 1972), p. 1; cf. Garrett Hardin, "Abortion vs. the Right to Life: The Evil of Mandatory Motherhood," *Psychology Today* (November 1974), pp. 42–43.

75. Ibid., p. 3.

76. Ibid., p. 4. Since I wrote this book, a sequel to Joseph Fletcher's original article was published. Cf. "Four Indicators of Humanhood—The Enquiry Matures," *Hastings Center Report* (December 1974), pp. 4–7. Professor Fletcher has now listed the criteria "as the singular *esse* of humanness: neo-cortical function, self-consciousness, relational ability, and happiness" (p. 5).

77. Dyck, *Religious Views,* p. J-22.

78. Ibid., p. J-60.

79. Ibid., pp. J-61–62; cf. David J. Bleich, "Abortion in Halakhic Literature," *Tradition* X, no. 2 (1968) pp. 72–120; cf. Immanuel Jacobovits, *Jewish Medical Ethics* (New York: Bloch, 1967); cf. Isaac Klein, "Abortion and Jewish Tradition," *Conservative Judaism* XXIV, no. 3 (1970), pp. 26–33.

80. Dyck, *Religious Views,* pp. J-58–J-60.

81. *Congressional Quarterly,* May 16, 1974, p. 681.

82. Ibid.

83. I am referring to Stanley Hauerwas's use of "story." Cf. "Love's Not All You Need," *Cross Currents* XXI, no. 4 (Fall 1971), and "Christian Ethics and the Humanization of Man: A Test Case for the Methodology of Theological Ethics," presented at Religion and the Humanizing of Man, International Congress of Learned Societies, in the field of religion, September 1–5, 1972, Century Plaza Hotel, Los Angeles.

84. Charles Hartshorne, "Ethics and the Process of Living," an unpublished paper presented at the conference Religion, Ethics and the Life Process, the Institute of Religion and Human Development, Texas Medical Center, March 18–19, 1974.

85. H. Tristram Engelhardt, Jr., "The Ontology of Abortion," *Ethics* LXXXIV, no. 3 (April 1974), p. 218; cf. Engelhardt, "The Process of

Embodiment and Bioethics," an unpublished paper presented at the Institute of Religion and Human Development, Texas Medical Center, March 18–19, 1974.

86. Ibid.

87. Ibid., p. 220.

88. Ibid., pp. 221–222. Cf. Ad Hoc Committee of the Harvard Medical School to Examine the Definition of Brain Death, "A Definition of Irreversible Coma," *Journal of the American Medical Association* (August 1968), pp. 85–88; Daniel Silverman, Michael G. Saunders, Robert S. Schwab, and Richard L. Masland, "Cerebral Death and the Electroencephalogram," *Journal of the American Medical Association* (September 8, 1968), pp. 1505–10.

89. Ibid., p. 223.

90. Ibid., p. 224.

91. Ibid., pp. 224–225.

92. Ibid., p. 228.

93. Ibid., pp. 227–228.

94. Sissela Bok, "Ethical Problems of Abortion," *Hastings Center Studies* II, no. 1 (January 1974), pp. 33–52.

95. Ibid., p. 36.

96. Ibid.

97. Ibid., p. 37.

98. Ibid., pp. 38–39.

99. Hartshorne, "Ethics and the Process of Living," p. 7.

100. Yamakami, *Systems of Buddhistic Thought*, p. 78.

101. John B. Cobb, Jr., *God and the World* (Philadelphia: Westminster Press, 1969), p. 135.

102. Alfred North Whitehead, *Religion in the Making* (Cleveland: World, 1966), p. 17.

103. Cf. David R. Griffin, *A Process Christology* (Philadelphia: Westminster Press, 1973), pp. 147–148. Professor Griffin outlines a large task.

> To support Christian existence we need 1) a means of judging the Christian view of things as essentially true, so that a complete relativism can be avoided; 2) a way of speaking of the reality and efficacy of those values fundamental to Christian existence; 3) a way of conceiving the reality of human freedom in relation both to other finite causes and to the divine causality; 4) a way of conceiving God's power so that the fact of evil does not falsify the Christian evaluation of God's character and purpose; 5) a way of conceiving God's power so that, further, the gradualness and particularity of God's self-revelation does not falsify the Christian evaluation of his character and purpose.

See also my review of *A Process Christology*, in *Horizons* (Fall 1974).

Reshaping Values:
Toward a Common Universe
Of Processive Man

Morality . . . is like a cultivated field at the edge of a desert, representing a "partial and precarious conquest," and requiring reorganization as conditions change. "In the last analysis all depends on the energy, perseverance, and perpetual vigilance of the human person."[1]

In the preceding chapters I have discussed a methodology for operational, process ethics. The focus of my concern has been the role of the bioethician. Because of the significance of the issue of the origin of life within the process of fetal development, the problematic of abortion was selected to illustrate a natural paradigmatic case for which religious paradigms and attendant constructs have been employed. Obviously, a conclusion to such an exploration is impossible. However, I would like to suggest the importance of a methodology for an operational, process ethics in the reshaping of values.

The operational hypothesis, i.e., "something is what it does," with which I have been working, suggests that a reconstruction of priorities in terms of functional value is necessary in relating to the contemporary bioethical issues which face the present and the future. It further suggests that issues may be simplified if they are looked at as complex, organic wholes which can be broken down if one adopts a processive world view. This method has also indicated that religion is a common experience out of which a common universe of discourse might be achieved when dealing with ethical issues of unprecedented significance. This will do no injustice to the realm of the "spiritual life" for in this realm each religion is distinct in what it suggests by way of individual and communal perfection. An ontology of human values—value ontology—provides a common ground of concern through which all men, regardless of individual and social commitments, may discuss the process of "making important," of deciding how to shape the "I" of their personal existence.

In order for this approach to be productive it must be communicated within an educational perspective which suggests a dynamic view of the nature of man in his environment. The value of the operational, process perspective lies in its power to transform and create new modes of functional worth. To create a "response of value" is the end product of this methodology. This response of value can only come about in a "field of focused relations." Contrary to behavioristic psychology, value ontology is significant only when connected and concretized by relations. Constructs, such as "the sanctity of life," and "the right to life," must be relationally centered if they are to be constructs and not simply concepts. An educational perspective must foster a respect for the issues themselves, whether we are concerned with abortion, "death with dignity," human experimentation, genetic engineering or genetic screening, as well as a respect for those with whom the issues are related. The common factor in the medical model of health, the psychological model of health, the religious model of well-being, and the spiritual model of salvation is WHOLENESS. Although each discipline is distinct in its concern, its common feature is wholeness.

Religious ethics, possessing a changing image as we move further into the twentieth century, creates the category of novelty as a necessary course of imaginative technique. Its search for renewed incentive and motivation reaches into individually and socially relevant data and needs. In the process of decision-making, man is addressed by the culture in which he actively lives and from which he consciously or unconsciously takes his cues. He is addressed through options which science and technology claim will improve his existence. Since he is a man in an age of precision, psychologically geared to eleminate undue suffering and want, he will listen to the options technique offers. However, unless he is able to establish a "standpoint" embodying both precision and personal value, science and technology will encourage impotence rather than an ability to respond with reshaped values to sustain both of his demands. A revitalized, i.e., an informed, standpoint toward these emerging concerns must be the goal of education. Responses of value may only be uttered and acted upon if they are informed.

Values are created. They derive their content from the issues which prompt antecedent values to surface. Values are the one commodity which man knows that he cannot afford to do without. Recent American history shows the bedlam which is created when values are tossed aside for individual power and prestige. Because man is in need of values, in many instances he has substituted traditional religion for any new efforts to reshape values. Religion, in its traditional forms intimately connected with the spiritual life and individual salvation, has attracted many who rest most comfortably in its offerings. Active decision-making has been left to bodies of institutional morality—the churches. Individual decision-making is possible by a literalization of laws and forms but highly improbable because the tools of decision-making—facts, options, consequences, relational quality, the place of memory, forgetfulness, imagination, "importance," and transcendence—are missing. Not knowing what to do and wanting to do something creates the ethical paradox. Among so many options the individual remains static in his impotence of will. I contend that the real issue is a lack of methodological know-how.

> Willingness to protect life as an individual understands it, and to protect the individual's conscientious choice, and the willingness to find a place for the weak, the infant and the aged, the crippled, the defective, mutilated by accident or war are a measure of a good society. But this is only so if this willingness is joined by the most vigorous attempt to abolish the conditions that make these decisions so paradoxical, contradictory and difficult.[2]

Within the process view of man-in-the-world decision-making and the creation of values, understanding the causative influence of human experience is important. Each individual is made up of a series of never-to-be-repeated experiences. However, each one influences the next. Professor Barbour explains:

> There is also an element of self-causation or self-creation, since every event unifies what is given to it by the past in its own manner from its unique perspective on the world. It contributes something of its own in the way it appropriates its past, relates itself to various possibilities, and produces a novel synthesis that is not strictly deducible from its antecedents. There is a creative selection from among alternative potentialities in terms of goals and aims, which is final causation. Every new occurrence can, in short, be looked on as a present response to past events in terms of potentialities grasped.[3]

A novel synthesis is the result of each event constituted by the decision-making process. Values are then shaped to fit the emerging situation in an ontological context. This involves phenomenology of making important, as Professor Whitehead suggests. In the end it is the only recourse for a people limited by their own inventiveness.

In the preceding chapters I have said little about the construct "God." I do not think that much needs to be said. By the process I have unfolded I have already located the function of the God construct. It is the process itself. "God" is the persuasive force of possibility and the restraining force of limitation. The imagination of man in its holistic appreciation of biomedical issues does not need the category of God in order to see the need and the demand for virtue. The power of the concern itself is immediately translated into ultimate terms by the individual or the society which faces it. I do not do "God" or man any justice by artificially introducing the obvious. The goal of harmony amid the ethical paradox speaks for itself. The "gods" of men's spiritual traditions will emerge and force a transcendence of "god." "God" as an operable construct will emerge from the natural paradigms of biomedical issues in the form of ultimate questions which both push man further into scientific endeavors and also further into knowledge of the transcendent meaning of such ventures. "God" encompasses the ethical paradox for it is this construct which is created by man to couch the mysteries of his life and thoughts. Although the construct "God" may be a different emphasis or focus in the distinct religious traditions, the common language of "ultimate significance in a finite world" has a universal response of value in the ethical realm.

A final note: Religious ethics as embodied in the role of the ethician is the relevant force of the next decade. As America settles into a quiet period of serious recuperation, the emphasis will be on solving the dilemmas which have been put aside while other matters drew our attention. A more conservative attitude will be felt, but this should not mean that we must retain religious paradigms which are inoperative. Perhaps this time of serious study will reflect an equally valid effort in the search for a common universe of processive man in the biomedical areas. Through a deliberate effort, religious ethics will place its emphasis on the broken perspective of man free to rebuild a realistic vision of man amid the ethical paradox. Contradiction and failure will never be entirely dismissed. Yet, the power of organization may create such a condensation of energy that individual decision-making will be rendered a natural part of the process, exemplified here by biomedical sciences.

The reconstruction of religious truth must seek this direction; religion cannot long survive only under the veil of "spirituality." The reshaping of our vision—including paradigms and constructs —is the obligation of the present for the future.

NOTES

1. Ralph B. Perry, *Realms of Value* (Cambridge: Harvard University Press, 1954), p. 100, as adapted and quoted in Eugene C. Conover, *Personal Ethics in an Impersonal World* (Philadelphia: Westminster Press, 1967), p. 148.
2. Margaret Mead, "Right to Life," *Christianity and Crisis* XXXII, no. 23 (June 8, 1973), p. 291.
3. Ian G. Barbour, *Myths, Models and Paradigms: A Comparative Study in Science and Religion* (New York: Harper & Row, 1974), p. 163.

Date Due

BJJJ